A WHOLE NEW ERA

Emerging Apostles
and Prophets Today

Bruce Lindley

Foreword by Ché Ahn

A Whole New Era – Emerging Apostles and Prophets Today
by R. Bruce Lindley

Published by
ARC Global
PO Box 4393
Helensvale B.C. QLD 4212
Australia

This book or parts thereof may not be reproduced in any form, stored in a retrieval system, or transmitted in any form by any means – electronic, mechanical, photocopy, recording or otherwise – without prior written permission of the publisher, except as provided by Australian copyright law.

All scripture quotations are from the New International Version 2011 of the Bible unless otherwise specified. HOLY BIBLE, NEW INTERNATIONAL VERSION. Copyright © 2011 by Zondervan. Used by permission of Zondervan. All rights reserved.

Copyright © 2020 Bruce Lindley

Cover design by Rachel Lindley

ISBN: 978-0-9942402-3-1

Printed in Australia

Dedication

A Whole New Era is dedicated to our Lord and Savior who calls us into this New Era.

It is also dedicated to my precious wife Cheryl, who is an amazing example of a New Era prophet.

And it is dedicated to our spiritual sons and daughters. The world awaits as you emerge to transform the world for the Kingdom of God.

I especially dedicate this book to the remarkable apostles and prophets in our amazing apostolic community ARC Global. What an honor it is to discover and implement this new wineskin with you. We get to Go and transform the world for the Kingdom of God together.

Acknowledgements

This book wouldn't have been possible without the support and help of my amazing Cheryl Lindley. And to our wonderful Apostolic Restore Community (ARC) Global family.

Special thanks to Carol Martinez for her wonderful editing skills.

Contents

    Foreword by Ché Ahn..7

    Introduction..11

1. Big Picture – A New Wineskin............................17
2. A Whole New Era..33
3. Apostolic and Prophetic Leadership Overview..47
4. Function, Not Title 57
5. How Do We grow New Wineskin Apostles and Prophets?. 67
6. The Heart and Values of Apostles and Prophets. ..85
7. Apostolic Alignment. 103
8. What Is an Apostolic Community?....................117
9. Co-Missioning 127
10. ARC Global's Apostolic Community 137

    Endnotes..143

Foreword

by Ché Ahn

I have had the privilege of personally knowing Bruce for over three decades. As the years have gone by, I have seen the fruit borne in his life on a personal level as well as in the realm of ministry.

Ten years ago, I had the honor of commissioning Bruce and Cheryl as apostles, as a part of Harvest International Ministry, recognizing that they both carry the biblical DNA of the fivefold as they equip and launch emerging prophetic and apostolic leaders in the Body of Christ. Bruce truly has a heart for transformation and lives with a sure commitment to see the Kingdom of God advanced throughout Australia and all over the world. I am grateful to God that I can call Bruce a spiritual son and a very good friend.

If you look at what is taking place on the global stage right now, I think everyone would agree that we are living in extraordinary times. Wherever you may live around the world, one thing is certain: God is doing a new thing, and we need to be part of it!

With his new book, *A Whole New Era*, Bruce Lindley invites each one of us to step into the fulness of what God has prepared for the global Church in this exciting New Era. I believe we are witnessing a restoration of God's original intent for the Body of Christ as ministers of the Gospel are embracing the complete fivefold ministry, with appropriate emphasis on the importance of apostles and prophets (Ephesians 2:20). In down-to-earth and relational terms, Bruce presents a clear understanding of how we can mold our ministries and mindsets to respond to how the Spirit of God is moving among the nations.

Right now, each one of us has the opportunity to catch the vision and learn what we can do to walk in the new wineskin that God has prepared for His Church.

This book may challenge your preconceived ideas of what ministry is supposed to look like, and if so, I believe it will replace those ideas with a refreshing new perspective that is based on the Word of God.

Bruce lives this message, and he aptly applies Scripture with direct relevance for the prophetic time frame we have entered in Church history. You and I were created to live out the truth of Scripture with Spirit-empowered effectiveness in our ministries and our personal lives. When we allow God to transform us personally, we will be able to transform our cities and, ultimately, our nations.

Fivefold ministers are marked by the Father's heart for the next generation, and this book is in sync with that spiritual calling. The apostles that God commissions are being

FOREWORD

sent to bring Heaven's culture to transform the current cultural landscape around the world, and together with prophets and the other fivefold members, we will collectively help to fulfill the Great Commission and disciple nations by the grace and power of God.

Take these words to heart and let the Holy Spirit expand your capacity to walk in your God-given authority and divine destiny on the earth. We have the opportunity to partner with Heaven's agenda for this New Era in the Kingdom, and I am convinced that we will see the glory of God cover the earth and bring about a Great Harvest that the world has never before seen.

Ché Ahn
Founder and President,
Harvest International Ministry
Founding and Senior Pastor,
Harvest Rock Church, Pasadena, CA
International Chancellor, Wagner University
Founder, Ché Ahn Ministries

Introduction

We are in a period of dramatic change in the world right now! As I write this Introduction, the world is in the grip of one of the worst pandemics experienced in most people's lifetime – Corona Virus (COVID 19). It is extremely contagious and sadly, people from every nation are dying in large numbers.

Nations are closing their borders, international flights are grounded, travelers from overseas are quarantined, people are panic buying food, businesses are closing and employees are having to work from home. Sporting events have been cancelled and people gathering in large numbers are outlawed. So much so that churches are no longer able to meet together on Sundays for worship.

One of the few positives from all of this is that suddenly the church of Jesus Christ has to look for different ways to have church – whether it is by 'streaming' online or by using other creative new ways of doing church.

My sense is that things will change permanently once this pandemic is over – and we have a choice to step into this change now.

One of the keys to life is that you need to change with the changes around you. In fact, change is important, because it is necessary for you and me to fulfil our God purpose.

But what we are experiencing right now is dramatic change.

Sometimes in history there is accelerated change. We are in such a time today.

The truth is that even without taking into account the Corona Virus, we are living in a time of perhaps the greatest change. So, we have to change whether we like it or not.

Many prophets and Christian leaders have been declaring over the last few years that this time is in fact A whole 'New Era'.

What Is a New Era? What Does that Look Like?

This book, *A Whole New Era – Emerging Apostles and Prophets Today,* examines just that.

Up until now, most Christian leaders have used the term 'new season' to try describing change in their world.

But a 'New Era' is very different from a 'new season'. As long as I can remember, leaders have been saying, 'It is a new season,' but we are entering into much more than a 'new season'.

When society changes and you do not change, you will be left behind. It is not change for change's sake.

INTRODUCTION

As Christians, we have an advantage because we have already experienced transformation — when we were born again in Christ. For me, everything changed from that time on.

So, we should be willing to step into this New Era quickly. For Christians, it's about changing along with what God is doing and has already done.

History shows us that the body of Christ is not good at this. That's what religion did at the time of Jesus and that is what religion does to us now.

So, this New Era has to be supernatural or it simply won't last. God's people will reset back to what they have always done. They will just re-badge titles and change their jargon.

You can change the outside, but what good is that if there is no real change in you?

> *When everything else is changed around you and you don't change... You get left behind.*

Why change is necessary

Jesus is the ultimate change. He is still the hinge of history. Up until recently, everything was dated either BC or AD (Before Christ and Anno Domini or After Christ).

So, the greatest change agent still wants to change us. His power is still moving us from being conformed to the pattern of this world of old mindsets to being transformed by the renewing of our minds (Romans 12:2) – into new wineskin; thinking and living in this New Era.

In a New Era, everything changes!

Our challenge is to recognize that things have changed whether we want to change or not!

When there is change, there are always early adopters followed by the majority who eventually end up changing too! Normally, this takes time.

Occasionally, dramatic change comes at a point of time like now, whether we like it or not.

I remember this happening when I was a boy in Australia, when our nation changed its currency from pounds to dollars on a single date.

On 14 February 1966, a decimal currency, the dollar of one hundred cents, was introduced into Australia, replacing the old currency of pounds, shillings and pence.

Everything was priced in dollars and cents from that day forward.

Now, there was plenty of advertising and education over three years leading up to that day, and the old currency was still valid for a few more years before it was phased out altogether. But eventually, the old currency didn't work anymore.

We are in such a time of transition in the body of Christ right now. You may still be using the old currency or old wineskin, but eventually the old currency won't work anymore.

INTRODUCTION

A Whole New Era — Emerging Apostles and Prophets Today has been written to resource you into this New Era.

It is an overview of the manual that has been put together from a two-day event that I have been running now since 2017 for Emerging Apostles and Prophets in Australia and in South East Asia to resource you and other emerging apostles and prophets into this New Era.

Are you willing to change and step into this New Era that God has begun?

My prayer is that you will be by the time you have finished reading this book!

CHAPTER 1

Big Picture – A New Wineskin

This is a time of significant change. The change is so substantial that it is equivalent to the change that brought about the Reformation and the subsequent changes that shifted our world. That change was so great that all of church history has since shifted from that point onwards.

We are at such a time in history again.

One of the greatest challenges for the church of Jesus Christ is that we don't tend to respond quickly when change comes. We are not normally early adopters. Change tends to happen slowly in the church.

As long as I can remember, I have read, heard and also spoken about our need for revival and awakening in our society, nation and the world.

But to have true revival, a new wineskin to hold the next outpouring of the Holy Spirit is needed.

Why?

Well, Jesus said so in Mark 2:21-22:

'No one sews a patch of unshrunk cloth on an old garment. Otherwise, the new piece will pull away from the old, making the tear worse. And no one pours new wine into old wineskins. Otherwise, the wine will burst the skins, and both the wine and the wineskins will be ruined. No, they pour new wine into new wineskins'.

A new wineskin is needed today.

When God pours out His spirit, we will not be able to contain it if we are still the same.

We will not be able to flow in this New Era if we are still an old wineskin.

Notice what I said—*We are the wineskin.* So, I'm not talking about church structures. We, the body, are the ones who need to change!

If we don't, then we will not be able to contain the new wine of God's outpouring.

Paul said it this way in 2 Corinthians 5:17:

'Therefore, if anyone is in Christ, the new creation has come: The old has gone, the new is here!'

The immediate context of this passage is the need for us, as individuals, to be born again. When that happens, our spirit man is reborn, and you come alive to God. Everything changes. You move from death to life. Your mindset and how you think changes. Your values and morals change. Not because you have to, but because you want to now please God.

The wider context is that this principle is also very important for the body of Christ. You have to understand that everything in society has changed.

The old wineskin has changed. As C. Peter Wagner says,

> *'The Church Age is now over.*
> *The new Kingdom age has begun'.* [1]

The truth is, the old wineskin of doing church does not work well anymore. Yes, there are some exceptions. But generally, most Christian leaders using an old wineskin are frustrated because what they have always done is no longer working the way it used to.

It is not just the church age that has since changed in this New Era. The whole world has changed.

Society has dramatically changed in this social media age. We now have instant communication around the world. We have instant access to the world as it changes.

And we're able to communicate with people on the other side of the world in real time now.

In fact, sometimes if you take more than an hour to respond to your message or email, people wonder what is wrong.

This has had huge ramifications for the way we do church.

For example, Christians now have constant access to feed themselves online with biblical teaching and worship; it's right at their fingertips whenever they want it. While we still believe in the need for Christians to be a part of a church, the truth is that many are no longer dependent on receiving their teaching through a Sunday sermon. If the church fails to recognize this and keeps using the old model (wineskin) of ministry, they will continue to be discouraged and lack impact on society.

But something much more dramatic than this has taken place.... God has brought into place a new wineskin in the Kingdom of God.

And the old wineskin just does not work anymore!

Why? It is the time of a New Era.

In Galatians 4:4 Paul says,

'But when the set time had fully come.... God sent forth his son'.
This new wineskin is our set time!

> *This is more than a whole new season.*
> *It is a whole New Era.*

The New Era has fully come. A New Era has come to birth.

It truly is a whole NEW ERA (See more about what the New Era is in Chapter 2.)

This new wineskin is also a Re-Formation.

Ephesians 2:19-20 says it this way,

'Consequently, you are no longer foreigners and strangers, but fellow citizens with God's people and also members of his household, built on the foundation of the apostles and prophets, with Christ Jesus himself as the chief cornerstone.'

One of the most important parts of this re-formation is that there has been a restoration of the five offices or foundational gifts to the body of Christ found in Ephesians 4:11-13:

'So Christ himself gave the apostles, prophets, the evangelists, the pastors and teachers, to equip his people for works of service, so the body of Christ may be built up until we all reach unity in the faith and in the knowledge of the son of God and become mature, attaining to the whole measure of the fullness of Christ.'

It began in the 1920s with the restoration of the office of the evangelist. A man called Billy Sunday was the first to introduce the concept of altar calls. He held his revival meetings in big tents that had sawdust floors. And at the end of his preaching he would call people to 'hit the sawdust trail' and come forward and give their lives to Jesus.

Billy Sunday was the forerunner of the office of the evangelist being restored to the body of Christ. Soon after, many other evangelists began to come forth like Jack Coe, A.A.

Allen, Aimee Semple McPherson, and T.L. Osborn. It culminated in 1947 with the launching of Oral Roberts' healing ministry and Billy Graham evangelism crusades that spread all around the world over the next 70 years. Many other evangelists came forth during this time, such as Reinhard Bonnke, who saw 79 million people come to Christ through his ministry in his lifetime.

God had restored the office of the Evangelist to the body of Christ.

In the 1950s and 60s, there was another office restored to the body of Christ. It was the office of the Teacher.

A fivefold Teacher is one who can impart biblical truths that can be easily understood by members of the body of Christ.

While there had been teachers prior to this, most of it was in the form of expository preaching. Charles Spurgeon was known as the prince of preachers and an amazing teacher. However, it was primarily in the form of a preaching gift.

Suddenly in the 1950s and 60s, teachers like Derek Prince, David Pawson and John Stott from England came forth, along with many teachers in the USA like Dick Iverson, Frank Damazio, Don Basham, John Osteen, Gwen Shaw, and our own Kevin Conner from Australia.

But the most well-known example was the Word of Faith movement. Kenneth Hagin Senior, known as the father of this Word of Faith movement, and Kenneth Copeland were the most well-known pioneers. They were at the forefront of a new emphasis of teaching the principles of faith and the Word of God using conferences, teaching series, and daily television programs to teach the body of Christ. Kenneth Copeland still sees his primary gift as a teacher to the body of Christ.

Other mainline churches also began to recognize the importance of all those with a true teaching gift. No longer were teachers being confined to overseeing Adult Sunday School programs or Bible studies for small groups. The office of the Teacher had been restored to the body of Christ.

Then in the 1970s, God restored the office of the Pastor. Obviously, there had been many ministers and clergy prior to this who had practiced pastoral care. But suddenly, in the midst of the Charismatic Renewal of the 1960s, 70s and 80s, there was an overflow of Christians experiencing the baptism in the Holy Spirit and being equipped to go into the ministry in large numbers. As a result, many of the Pentecostal and Evangelical movements began to train and mobilize church planters and pastors. Consequently, there was an influx of a large number of pastors in the body of Christ around the world. The unfortunate outcome was that we began to call everyone 'pastor' whether they had that gift or not.

Those in the true office of the Pastor have a shepherd's heart; they live to care for God's people and desire to see them grow up in Christ and fulfil God's destiny for their lives.

One of the challenges that came out of the restoration of the office of the Pastor was that it became a pattern to ordain all those in ministry as pastors and call everyone by that title whether they were in the office of the Pastor or not.

So, unfortunately, the title of Pastor has been used wrongly in the body of Christ. Instead of recognizing all of the separate offices of the fivefold we have ordained all apostles, prophets, evangelists, and teachers as pastors.

This is a challenge of the old wineskin that we are still dealing with today.

Then in 1980s and 90s, the office of the prophet was restored to the body of Christ.

Unfortunately, prior to this, the office of the prophet had not been widely recognized since the early church. Most believed that the office of the prophet and the apostle ceased after the Book of Acts and the establishment of the early church. And if you did operate as a prophet, you were largely ostracized, and at worst, accused of operating in the spirit of witchcraft.

But God used the Charismatic renewal of the 1970s and 80s to reintroduce the gift of prophecy.

According to of Acts 2 you can't experience the baptism of the Holy Spirit without your sons and daughters prophesying.

As it was practiced and mentored in the 1980s and 90s, the office of the prophet began to be recognized and come forth.

The father of the modern prophetic movement, Bishop Bill Hamon, wrote an amazing book on prophecy called *Prophets and Personal Prophecy — God's Prophetic Voice Today* in 1987.[2] It was instrumental in restoring personal prophecy to the body of Christ and restoring the office of prophet. It is still a classic reference book today.

After that, God raised up some amazing prophets like James Goll and the Kansas City prophets, Patricia King, Cindy Jacobs and many more. So much so, that an Apostolic Council of Prophetic Elders (ACPE) and a Global Prophetic Movement from 44 nations were established. They meet yearly to pray, wait on God together, and release what God is saying to the body of Christ around the world for that New Year. In addition, ministries like Elijah House have given emerging prophets all around the world a platform for publishing prophetic words. What was unheard of in the 1970s and 80s, the office of the prophet is now widely regarded as an important part of the body of Christ today.

Then in the decade of 2000, God restored the office of the apostle to the body of Christ. This restoration of the apostle has been the most significant for the implementation of this new wineskin in the New Era

What is an apostle? Here is the best explanation I have seen.

> 'Apostles today do all that is practiced in the book of Acts – preach the gospel with signs and wonders, establish and oversee churches. And most importantly, they are spiritual fathers. They raise up next generation sons and daughters'. [3]

The most radical change is in apostolic leadership. We will talk more about that in a later chapter on The Heart and

Values of Apostles and Prophets. But this is one of the major characteristics of this new wine skin.

One of the greatest challenges to the implementation of this new wineskin is that the majority of the church has only recognized three of the fivefold offices — the Pastor, the Evangelist and the Teacher.

As Bill Hamon wisely explains 'We normally accept ministerial church order, structure and relationships from these three but have mostly excluded the function and ministry of the apostles and prophets'. [4]

Instead, the old wineskin has called all of these offices by one title – Pastor. So instead of having a five-fingered hand. We have one-finger hand to oversee the body of Christ.

But this is what has changed in this New Wineskin:

As Peter Wagner says,

'Apostles and prophets did not finish their task after the first century of the Christian movement, rather their ministry has never ceased throughout the world history of the church. Not all churches today recognize this true biblical government of the church, but those who do constitute the new wineskin for churches of the foreseeable future'. [5]

The truth is, there is nothing new under the sun. This is always how the church was supposed to operate. God has simply restored His divine order to the body of Christ.

So, this New Era is a Re-formation.

The foundations have been restored. Paul is quite clear about this in Ephesians 2:19-20:

'Consequently, you are no longer foreigners and strangers, but fellow citizens with God's people and also members of his household, built on the foundation of the apostles and prophets, with Christ Jesus himself as the chief cornerstone'.

God has restored the foundation of the apostles and prophets on which He can build his body of Christ.

A New Mind-Skin

This re-formation is much more than a restoration! It actually is a whole new wineskin.

We need to perceive the new wineskin by the Holy Spirit. And we have to catch it rather than merely have it taught to us. As 1 Corinthians 2:13-16 says,

> *We need*
> *spiritual realities with Spirit-taught words...*

'This is what we speak, not in words taught us by human wisdom but in words taught by the Spirit, explaining spiritual realities with Spirit-taught words. The person without the Spirit does not accept the things that come from the Spirit of God but considers them foolishness and cannot understand them because they are discerned only through the Spirit...'

Verse 16 goes on to say...

'But we have the mind of Christ'.

So, we need the mind of Christ before we can have a new wineskin.

Because the new wineskin is in fact a new 'Mind-Skin'.

In other words, the new wineskin is not a new structure but a new way of thinking!

> Our New Wineskin definition is = A new way of thinking that steers the body of Christ toward this New Era in God.

It requires a radical change in how apostolic and prophetic leaders think and act.

So as apostolic and prophetic leaders in the body of Christ, we need to take a step back and each ask God to 'show me any old wineskin thinking in me'.

My wife and I have been living this way since 2015 and I still find myself occasionally responding or thinking through an old wineskin mindset. In other words, it takes time to come out of the old and into the new.

I have decided that I'm so determined to live with a new wineskin mindset that I welcome my peers to challenge me if they hear me speaking any old wineskin concepts or operating out of an old mindset in our Apostolic Community.

Once you've made the decision to step into new wineskin, everything begins to change.

In fact, you will have to unlearn a lot of your models of ministry and how you have taught churches and leaders to operate.

I'm having to unlearn church growth concepts, models of ministry, ways of leadership as well as ways of thinking. This new wineskin is a whole new mind-skin for the body of Christ.

One of the greatest changes that takes place in us is that we have moved from being ministry or purpose-driven to a Spirit-led ministry model.

Jesus lived this way. In John 5:19, He said,

'I only do what I see my father doing'.

In other words, Jesus always looked for what his Father was blessing and only did that.

As well, Romans 8:15 tells us those who are led by the Spirit of God are sons of God. So, if we want to be Spirit-led, Spirit-controlled and have the mind of Christ in this new wineskin, we need to start living this way.

Another important aspect of this new wineskin is that everyone's wineskin looks different.

So, we should no longer be copying other people's models of ministry. Be yourself. Be secure in your own mind-skin and wineskin.

For we all have different spheres of influence and roles of transformation. No one's ministry is the same. No one else has the same gift mix as you do.

There is no one else like you!

Paul says it this way in Ephesians 4:7,

'But to each one of us grace has been given as Christ apportioned it'.

The word 'grace' or 'gift' here in Greek is the word '*metron*' which means a specific 'sphere of influence'.

God has given to each one of us a specific sphere of influence and authority that only we can fulfill. Your 'metron' is a unique social group, city, region, a state, nation or mountain of influence.

To step into the fulness of your sphere of influence using your new mind skin/wineskin, you have to first take off the old mindset.

This is only possible if you come out of religion; all the old ways of doing church. You have to go after the religious spirit in you. Relax, we all have it. We each have to recognize it and ask God to break us out of it.

We have to watch our words and our opinions of others who are doing ministry differently from us. And we need to let others help us by giving them permission call out the old wineskin in us.

The truth is, we can't do it ourselves. We need the Holy Spirit and the breaker anointing of 2 Samuel 5:20:

'So, David went to Baal Perazim, and there he defeated them. He said, "As waters break out, the Lord has broken out against my enemies before me."'

> *The breaker anointing allows the Father to break IN to our old mind skin so he can break us OUT into the new wineskin!*

The truth is, now is the time to make a decision to do this. This is the way He always intended you build the Kingdom of God.

The good news is that everyone is progressing in their own new wineskin journey. And there is great grace towards where you are right now. The key is not to look at what others are doing, but to invite the Father to send the breaker anointing to set you free from old mindsets, so you can walk in the fulness of this new wineskin.

CHAPTER 2

Whole New Era

It is interesting that when God does a new thing, even secular society begins to pick up on it and start talking about it. This has been especially true about this New Era.

More and more, people in different spheres of society are using 'New Era' as part of their terminology to describe something that is happening that is completely different and is some new way of practice which they have never seen or done before.

There is a simple reason for this.

It is a whole New Era.

Whether you're a Christian or not, the world has moved into a New Era.

It is much more than the latest trend or terminology. Something significant has changed.

Have you noticed that even the media, sport, business, and politics are all using the term 'New Era' as they seek to explain how they believe that many spheres of society are changing dramatically?

For generations, Christians preached, prophesied and declared that each year was a new season. Well, the Word of God says just that. Isaiah 43:18-19 declares:

'Forget the former things; do not dwell on the past.
See, I am doing a new thing!
Now it springs up; do you not perceive it?'

I love new seasons. Especially springtime and summer because there is always new life in nature around you. The challenge is that there are four new seasons each year. So, we are always having a new season. What is true in the natural is also true in the spiritual realm.

What is happening now in the Kingdom of God is much more than just a new thing or a new season.

> *If it is a New Era, it is up to us to see and perceive or understand what God is indeed doing.*

What is a New Era?

Unlike a new season, *Webster's Dictionary* defines a New Era as:

'an extended period of time usually characterized by a distinctive development or by a memorable series of events' [1]

So, a New Era is not a short period time or trend. It is over an extended long period of time, even up to hundreds of years.

In January 2020, Britain finally exited the European Union after 47 years of membership in the European economic and political union along with 27 other European nations. It took great turmoil, street protests, two national votes and cost two prime ministers their leadership. Brexit was a massive social upheaval of the present and a huge change of direction for Britain. On that day, their prime minister Boris Johnson declared, 'This is a moment of real national renewal and change. This is the dawn of a New Era...'

He understood that this decision was a major shift that would last for generations ... it truly has ushered that nation into a whole New Era!

So, we do not use this term 'New Era' lightly. It is a time of great change or distinctive developments.

> *We have begun a New Era in the body of Christ.*

Another word for era is 'epoch'. Now, we don't use the word 'epoch' much anymore in the English language; however, it still has a very powerful meaning.

The dictionary defines an 'epoch' as a long period of time, especially one in which there are new developments and great change. [2]

There Are Important Characteristics of a New Era

First, it is a long-extended period of time.

It is certainly not a few months or years or even decades long. It often lasts for hundreds of years. This was certainly the case for the Reformation which began in October 1517 and lasted for 500 years.

And it involves significant new development in the Kingdom of God.

C. Peter Wagner described this New Era as the New Apostolic Reformation. He called it the 'most significant change since Luther nailed his theses on the door of the Wittenberg Cathedral on October 31st, 1517 that began the Reformation'. [3]

So, a New Era or epoch always involves 'great change'.

How amazing is this?

We are in the beginning of a new period of history right now! And you have the opportunity to be on the cutting edge of it.

Another synonym for the word 'era' is the word 'age.'

Webster's Dictionary defines 'age' as:

'the time of life at which some particular qualification, power, or capacity arises or rests (turning 21, able to vote)'

And,

'a cultural period marked by the prominence of a particular item (entering the Reformation age)' [4]

The challenge for Christians is that popular culture has highjacked this term to describe the 'New Age' movement.

The New Age movement spread in the 1970s and '80s. Supposedly, it offered enlightenment and mystical knowledge through ancient Gnosticism, which is a form of the occult. It was fast-growing because it emphasized the metaphysical but was outside the mainstream of religion, and it allowed followers to live without any sort of moral accountability.

Thus, I thought 'New Age' terminology presented a challenge to Christians in describing the New Era until I had a conversation with my daughter Sarah Cheeseman, who is a remarkable next-generation prophetic leader. As we were discussing this concept together, she said, 'It is 'new age'…. but this is a 'New Age of Glory. I instantly knew she was right! So...

What does this New Age of Glory look like?

Like any change, it often unfolds around you before you can see it.

This is what has been happening since 2015.

You can't see it initially as you are in the midst of it! As it unfolds, more and more people begin to see that things are changing, and they begin to have clarity as to what is happening.

That's what took place on the 31st of October 2017, when many prophets decreed on the 500th anniversary of the Reformation that a whole New Era had begun.

As in the Reformation, this New Era is a time of significant change!

Whenever there is a New Era, there is a release of a whole new level of glory of the Holy Spirit,

The apostle Paul says it clearly in 2 Corinthians 3: 9:
'If the ministry (old era) that brought condemnation was glorious, how much more glorious is the ministry (New Era of glory) that brings righteousness!'

Verse 10 says,
'For what was glorious has no glory now in comparison with the surpassing glory (of this New Era).'

This a New Glory that is available to you in the New Era. As 2 Corinthians 3:11 says,
'And if what was transitory came with glory, how much greater is the glory of that which lasts'.

> *There is a greater glory for you in this New Era.*

But the key is not being satisfied with your current level of spiritual encounter or glory that you live in. This is the true context of verse 17.

'Now the Lord is Spirit, and where the Spirit of the Lord is, there is freedom'.

It has nothing to do with freedom in corporate worship. It has everything to do with freedom to experience new levels of glory in this New Era.

Paul sums it up for us in verse 18:

'And we all, who with unveiled faces contemplate the Lord's glory, are being transformed into his image with ever-increasing glory, which comes from the Lord, who is the Spirit'.

So you have entered into a New Era—whether you have realized this previously or not.

New Revelation and New Wineskins

The way this new glory manifests is through new revelation and a whole new wineskin of how the Kingdom of God now operates.

I have a saying in this New Era – 'I disagree with me'.

What does this mean?

It means that because there is so much new revelation and new wineskin, I have to disagree with my former paradigms and be open to the new. This New Era opens up revelation and wineskins for generations to come.

However, what we see as 'new' is actually the way that Jesus always intended His church to operate from the very beginning. This is exactly what Paul says in Ephesians 2: 19-20:

'Consequently, you are no longer foreigners and strangers, but follow citizens with God's people and also members of his household, built on the foundation of the **apostles and prophets**, with Christ Jesus himself as the chief cornerstone'.

> *Jesus Christ is the foundation of this New Era and new wineskin.*

Renaissance and Reformation

A great example of the sought change that is coming in this New Era was what took place in the Renaissance.

The Renaissance was a period of cultural, artistic, political and economic rebirth following the Middle Ages. It was credited with bridging the gap between the Middle Ages and modern-day era. And like all New Eras, it lasted a long period of time. It began in the 14th century in Italy and lasted well into the 17th century and spread all throughout Europe.

Even though it was known as a cultural movement, it was also the beginning of a new emphasis of thought which questioned and challenged religion and the role of the Catholic Church. It was in the midst of this that Luther and the Protestant Reformation came forth.

Like all New Eras, one of the things which characterized the Renaissance was a flourishing of art, literature, architecture and science. As well as intellectual thinkers expressing new ideas, there was a surge in explorers leading to significant exploration and discoveries of the New World by Christopher Columbus, Magellan, Marco Polo, Sir Walter Raleigh and many others.

This New Era became known as the Age of Discovery and resulted in new trading and shipping routes to the Americas, India and what is known as the Caribbean today.

One of the manifestations of a New Era is new expressions of creativity and revelation and new understanding of how to 'do' kingdom.

I've always said that Christians should be on the cutting edge of creativity as we have the source of all inspiration, the Holy Spirit, living within us. So, it is no surprise that the Christians in this New Era should be at the forefront of inventions, new technologies.

Some of the greatest inventors in history were radical Christians in the forefront of their fields of study. Despite what historians now say, one of the most famous was Columbus who knew the world was not flat regardless of all those in the old wineskin predicting certain death if one ventured out and set off to discover the Brave New World.

New Sounds of Worship in this New Era

Another significant thing that accompanies new eras is that there is always a release of a new sound.

If you look at an overview when the greatest changes took place in society, you will see that there was also the introduction of new sounds.

Probably the most obvious modern example of new styles of music in recent history during the social change of the 1960s was the introduction of rock 'n' roll. Like all new eras, the origins of this music had existed ten to twenty years prior to this great cultural change by groups such as the Beatles and Elvis Presley, who both said they were greatly influenced by rhythm and blues and gospel of African American singers and musicians.

It has been interesting to hear about new teaching in Christian circles regarding the importance of new sounds and sound waves in the Spirit. None of this surprises me. If you study revival history, you will see that every time there was a new move of God, there was a new move of worship.

Some of the greatest hymns of our faith come out of those times. 'A Mighty Fortress is our God' was written by Martin Luther. Charles Wesley wrote thousands of new hymns in the midst of the Wesleyan revival. And of course, the Salvation Army brought forth a new sound in the form of a brass band. William Booth would use these bands on street corners and outside bars where they evangelized the drunkards and those who were down and out.

We saw that again in Charismatic Renewal decades of the 1960s, '70s and '80s with a whole new style of worship with 'Scripture in Song' led by Dave & Dale Garrett.[5] Many of those songs from that move of God we are still singing today.

> *Every time there was a new move of God, there was a new sound and a new wave of worship.*

And this is even true today with Hillsong, Bethel and others leading the way.

Often the body of Christ is slow catching up.

Typically, only those who are early adopters can prophetically see that God is introducing a New Era. They are at the forefront, bringing forth new wineskin revelation, and new sounds in worship.

Quite honestly, the rest of the body of Christ criticizes anything that's new. Typically, those on the cutting edge of the last move of God criticize anything that is different from their own experience. For those who will change, it normally takes five to ten years to get used to the idea and eventually adopt the new expression of God's kingdom.

But you don't have to be like that. You can decide to be an 'early adopter' and jump into this New Era right now.[6]

To do this you need to make a decision to step out of old cycles and old wineskins.

This is a very serious decision and requires conviction in your heart. It is equivalent to a deep work of repentance because you have to separate yourself from old ways of thinking and many of the things that you have been taught previously as a leader.

For that reason, I often lay hands on my own head and ask God to deliver me from old wineskin thinking and help me step into a new wineskin. The more you do this, the more you too will recognize the old wineskin thinking and mindsets that you still have.

Like I have shared, I am so determined to step out of the old that I also give others permission to bring correction and challenge if they hear me speaking old wineskins concepts. If you are bold enough, I would encourage you to do this as well.

Remember – the new wineskin is a 'new mind-skin'. It requires a whole new mindset.

New Realms and Levels of Glory Break Old Cycles and Old Wineskins

The good news is that the more you step into new wineskin thinking, the new level of glory that accompanies the new wineskin begins to break old cycles and the old wineskin off your thinking.

Dr. Bill Hamon called this New Era the 'Third Apostolic Reformation' in in his book *Apostles, Prophets and the Coming Move of God*. [7] He raised the 'new age of glory' bar when he decreed,

> 'No longer will only the 'anointed man or woman of God' get to minister.
> All of God's saints get to participate in God's kingdom...
> This is going to require a radical change in how apostolic leaders think and act!' [8]

You need to break out of old cycles. The good news is that the new realms of glory that come with this New Era will break off the old patterns of doing kingdom that are part of your old wineskin.

This is not just important for our own personal minis- try, but as we begin to mentor and equip and enable oth- ers together, we will all step into the fulness of this New Era wineskin.

Bill Hamon describes it this way:

'There is an emerging movement that will revolutionize the 21st century church. The last generation Church will have an Apostolic Reformation that will be as great as the first-generation apostolic movement. The first-generation church prophets & apostles laid the foundation of the church. Now the last day Apostolic reformation will put the final finishing touches on the church. It will also bring revolutionary changes like the protestant movement did in its day. The work of restoration will continue until members of Christ's body are taught, trained, activated and matured in manifesting their apostleship ministries...'[9]

> *A word of caution.*
>
> I have discovered that human nature resists change. The old wineskin is especially good at doing this. Unfortunately, there are some that will take a step further and criticize anything that is new and threatens the status quo. So be wise. Know when to speak and when to observe.

The good news is that God will bring others across your path that are also in the process of stepping into this New Era. This has been happening to me for over five years now. No matter where I go in the world, I hear emerging apostolic leaders sharing the same new wineskin principles. I often ask who they have listened to or read regarding this new wineskin and New Era.

Over and over the answer is the same...No one! The Holy Spirit has been teaching me or giving me this insight.

This convinced me the Lord is in this. As Revelation 3 and 4 says repeatedly,

'For them who have ears to hear, let them hear what the spirit is saying to the church'.

> *You have a choice today.*
> *Are you going to stay in the old or are you going to step into the fulness of this Whole New Era?*

CHAPTER 3

Function, not Title

Let someone else praise you, and not your own mouth. – Proverbs 27:2

This new wineskin in the New Era is all about function— not titles. It is your function, not your title, that is important.

This is still such a big issue for leaders in the body of Christ that I decided to write a whole chapter just on this subject.

Why?

Because human nature will want to call us back into a religious hierarchy of exalting some above others. Over and over we say that this new wineskin is not vertical but horizontal.

It's flat. As apostles, we are not supposed to be on the top of a leadership chain of command.

Ephesians 2:19-20 tells us that as apostles and prophets, you are foundational. You are supposed to be on the bottom, not on the top, looking down.

This New Era is an Apostolic Reformation. God is taking us back to His original intended purpose of how the body of Christ is supposed to function.

The main function of apostles and prophets is equip the body of Christ – to equip the body to bring it into alignment or realignment.

That is exactly what I am doing by addressing this issue of function, not title.

It is time that emerging apostles and prophets and leaders in the body of Christ cross this bridge.

We need to get set free from old wineskin terminology and titles. In this New Era, no one is considered 'better' than anybody else. It's all about mutual respect and celebration of each other's function as we build the Kingdom of God together.

In some ways, it's a blessing in disguise. Because the use of titles causes you to easily tell whether someone has stepped into the new wineskin or is still operating in an old wineskin.

One of the functions of the apostles is to be a father or mother. True fathers and mothers are sure of themselves. As Proverbs 27:2 says, they don't need others to praise them. If you are still using titles when you sign messages or introduce yourselves, you are still functioning in a religious old wineskin. It is time to pull the old wineskin down!

Jenny Hagar, an amazing apostle and a leader of the prayer movement in Australia, says that it is time for apostles, prophets and leaders in the body of Christ to have the spirit of Gideon and have the conviction and the boldness to first go into our Father's house to pull down the idol of self and ministry. This needs to happen before we will be able to transform the nations for the Kingdom of God. [1]

The term apostles 'sent one' and 'sent for a specific purpose' describes your function. Apostle is what you do. It is not your title.

Is there biblical proof of this? Absolutely!

If you read the opening paragraphs of all of Paul's letters in the new Testament, you will see over and over that he does not present himself with the title apostle. Instead he describes his function.

> Romans 1:1– 'Paul, a servant of Jesus Christ, called to be an apostle...'

Function, not Title!

> 1 Corinthians 1:1– 'Paul, called to be an apostle of Christ Jesus by the will of God...'

Function, not Title!

> Galatians 1:1– 'Paul, an apostle — sent not from men nor by a man but by Jesus Christ and God the Father...'

Function, not Title!

Colossians 1:1– 'Paul, an apostle of Christ Jesus by the will of God...'

Function, not Title!

Why do you need a title?

Even though it's a New Era, there are so many leaders who are using old wineskin titles and terminology. Paul told us to 'Follow my example as I follow the example of Christ'.

> *One of the major changes that you need to step into the new wineskin is to no longer use titles to describe yourself and others.*

The main response when we teach this is, 'But isn't it a matter of respect?'

The answer is No! True respect and honor are demonstrated by attitude and action.

My spiritual father Ché Ahn is an incredible apostle. Yet no one calls him Apostle Ché. He introduces himself only as Ché. Now many of his spiritual sons and daughters refer to him as Papa Ché but this is not his title... it is a term of endearment and expression of love from us to him.

Using titles and expecting others to call you by those titles is part of the vertical hierarchy of the old wineskin.

We have paid such a high price to bring in this new wineskin, we will continue to fight hard against the old in us creeping back.

This is one of the reasons why I don't have a business card. I introduce myself as Bruce Lindley. I purposely don't use a title. It is interesting to see the response I get especially in Africa and other Third World countries that are so steeped in the use of titles in their old wineskin religious hierarchy. It is always fascinating when they discover that I am apostle to see their attitudes change towards me.

Why?

Because they have an old wineskin leadership model. I am able to often use it as an example in our Emerging Apostles and Prophet Summits in those nations.

I've discovered that you cannot demand respect and honor. You earn it as a leader by your Christlike example and by laying down your life for others.

If you expect a title, then you are still an orphan; not a son or a daughter

The truth is those people who demand the use of titles really do have an orphan heart.

I have discovered that true apostles know they are! You know where you're going and how to do it. You seek only to honor God. You are not interested in gaining the approval or respect of man.

> *And most importantly, true apostles are **sons** of God.*

As sons of the Father, there is no need to seek to please God. Because as sons of God, they know that God is already pleased with them.

In my book, *The Father's Love – An Encounter with God the Father,* I described it this way.

'In the Hebrew culture they still have an initiation ceremony for boys who reach the age of 13 called a bar mitzvah. It is the recognition that a boy has become a man and can begin to be treated as an adult. Not only does the ceremony signify they are ready to participate in public worship but that they also begin to act on behalf of the family. In Jesus's time, after the boy's bar mitzvah, the father would take his son into the marketplace.

'The father would climb on to something high and get the attention of all those present and then declare something similar to this: 'This is my son who I love and with whom I'm well pleased. He is now a man. From now on when my son speaks, he speaks for me. When my son enters into business transactions, he is doing so with my full authority. What belongs to me belongs to him. When he gives his word it's as if I am giving my word.'

'Jesus had a similar experience at His water baptism. In Luke 3:21-22 we are told that when Jesus was baptized, heaven was opened and the Holy Spirit physically descended on him in the form of a dove. As a pastor, I prepared people for their own water baptism with this passage of Scripture for many years. I always taught them to expect the Holy Spirit to come upon them as they were baptized in water. But I now realize I was only teaching them half of what happened to Jesus at His baptism'.

'Luke 3:22– 'You are my son, whom I love, with you I am well pleased.'

'The Bible tells us that all present heard the Father's voice that day. Everyone present heard what He said to His son. The power and significance of this was not lost on them that day'.[2]

Notice Jesus didn't need to go around introducing Himself with a title after that experience!

Jesus didn't need to tell others that He was the Son of God.

He didn't need to introduce Himself or tell us what the Father had said about Him.

Jesus knew who He was! He knew what the Father thought of Him. His identity was sure.

I have discovered that when someone has truly encountered God, they are different. And when you meet them you can tell straightaway that they walk with God, because they carry His presence.

> *When you know that you are loved by the Father, you know that He is already pleased with you. It empowers you for ministry.*

It's all you need to step out in faith and be sent. You can fulfil your call just on that experience with the Father heart of God.

You can even live in the midst of the wilderness and demonic opposition when you know that the Father loves you and is pleased with you.

Then you know who you really are …Your identity is sure.

You are a son of God. You are a son of the Father!

That the best thing they can ever say about you.

That is the best thing that you can be known for… that you are a son of God.

Once you have that identity, you don't need titles or the admiration of others.

You know that your Father loves you and is pleased with you.

This is enough for you to function as his son or daughter! Out of that identity comes incredible power and authority.

Luke 4:1 tells us that..

'Jesus, full of the Holy Spirit, the Jordan and was led
by the spirit into the wilderness...'

After Jesus's encounter with the father heart of God, His identity and authority manifested powerfully.

God the Father will do the same for us!

This is what Romans 8: 14-15 truly means:

'For those who are led by the Spirit of God are the children of God.

'The Spirit you received does not make you slaves, so you live in fear again; rather, the Spirit you received brought about your adoption to Sonship and by him we cry Abba, Father.'

Other translations have replaced the word 'adoption' with the 'spirit of Sonship.'

So, when you know who you are and how to be led by the spirit of God as a son or a daughter, titles are insignificant.

You are healthy in your heart and you don't need others' approval. You already have the approval of your heavenly Father.

Thus, then your whole focus is your function.

You then can truly begin to be *a 'Sent one' for a specific purpose:*

To begin to be apostolic and transform culture.

To equip and train others to transform their world.

To take people out of their culture and help them begin to live out of a kingdom culture.

So, let's be bold and start a revolution in the body of Christ.

Decide that you no longer need to have a title. You already have the Father's heart and His approval. You are confident in your identity as a son of God.

Now take that step out of the old wineskin and begin to teach others that this New Era in the body of Christ is no longer about titles but what you do. It is time to function as emerging apostles and prophets!

CHAPTER 4

Apostolic and Prophetic Leadership Overview

On the 4th of July 2015, apostles and prophets were in our house of prayer praying together in preparation for our first commissioning of apostles at ARC Global the following day. A number of our prophets saw the same vision of the sun rising over the horizon. It was a new sunrise.

We knew the Lord was speaking to us about the whole body of Christ stepping into the fulness of this New Era.

In the vision, the light, heat, and the fire of the rising sun of this New Era was so bright in comparison to the light of the moon. We knew that the moon was a picture of the old wineskin. It was beautiful. But we realized that the body of Christ can get so enamored with a beautiful picture of the old era, yet there is no heat and no strong light in it anymore.

By comparison, the sun was releasing great heat. God was releasing the light of His new day —it indeed was a whole New Era. We knew that there was an anointing being released at ARC Global for this New Era.

God was saying not to hesitate any longer in stepping into this new wineskin.

It has been quite an adventure since that day when we said 'Yes'!

One of our prophets saw a plumb line, with the old wineskin plummeting before the Lord.

The introduction of this New Era would be like a nuclear melt down. We knew it couldn't be controlled once it started.

There was so much oil of the Holy Spirit being released that we knew that there was an overflow of grace for this New Era.

Foundations

Ephesians 2:20 makes it very clear that in this new wineskin we need to get our foundations right.

> *This New Era must be –*
> *built on the foundation of the apostles*
> *and prophets, with Christ Jesus himself as*
> *the chief cornerstone.*

The foundation of God's household is built on apostles and prophets.

As we discussed in Chapter 2, this New Era is an Apostolic Reformation. God has restored the Ephesians 4 role of apostles and prophets as well as the rest of the five governing gifts to function in the body of Christ.

So, apostles and prophets must take their place. The restoration of apostles and prophets will bring forth the greatest release of this New Era that we have ever seen.

The Key Function of Apostles and Prophets

The key function of apostles and prophets must be to transform communities, cities, regions and nations.

If apostles and prophets are foundational, then they need to address the existing foundations of the old wineskin. For the foundations to change from the old to the new, there needs to be a major transformation in the mindsets as well as the methodology of leaders and their leadership.

Alain Caron in his book describes apostles and prophets becoming 'Foundational De-constructionists and Re-constructionists. [1]

In this New Era, you will see a lot of new terminology as apostles and prophets attempt to describe what this wineskin looks like. I like that the New Era apostles are being described as 'foundational constructionists' because it offers a picture of what God is doing right now through His body around the world.

There will need to be a lot of deconstruction of the old before there can be a true moving into this New Era.

What is an apostle? C. Peter Wagner says,

'The apostle is a Christian leader, gifted, taught, commissioned and sent by God with the authority to establish foundational government of the Church within its assigned sphere of ministry by hearing what the Spirit is saying to the churches and by setting things in order accordingly for the expansion of the Kingdom of God'.[2]

As we will see, modern-day apostles are similar but different from the apostles in the book of Acts and the early church.

Chuck Pierce in his book *The Apostolic Church Arising* says that,

'The gift of apostle is a gift with a very specific function that only apostles can perform.

'Apostles establish the church. Apostles have a gift from God to create an administration with which other gifts can grow and develop. Apostles are key elements of God's order for His church. When apostles are functioning, you will see the fivefold come into its place. The saints are equipped, and the Kingdom of God will flourish'. [3]

One of the unique characteristics and changes of this new wineskin is the amount of authority that the Holy Spirit gives to individuals! As C. Peter Wagner says, this does take some getting used to but this New Era is the most radical change in doing church since the Protestant reformation. [4]

Compared to previous wineskins, in this New Era the elders' or board's role is to support the apostle's decisions. The reality is that it works best through an apostolic five-fold team. Their job is to equip and mobilize others to do the work of the ministry.

What does apostolic ministry look like?

Apostles see the big picture! They are visionaries, but they are also able to explain what they see in a practical way that others are easily able to also see and run with it. As well, they have the strategies to implement what God has spoken through the prophets.

Apostles and prophets work together.

Prophets hear and see the divine insights into what God is saying and doing, and God gives apostles strategies of the new things that God is releasing through His prophets.

Apostles also have the anointing to pull other leaders together and impart vision of this new wineskin to bring about significant change.

What is a prophet?

In Ephesians 2:20, Paul lists the office of a prophet as the second foundational gift.

Chuck Pierce says that:

'Prophecy is the ability to communicate the mind and heart of God in a specific situation'.[5]

All Christians should know how to prophesy. Acts 2:17 says just that as Peter quotes Joel's prophecy:

'I will pour out my Spirit on all people. Your sons and daughters will prophesy'.

God speaks to us all, and we all can learn to hear His voice. But just hearing God's voice does not make you a prophet. The main role of a prophet is to teach others to listen and hear God's word for themselves. One of their roles is to speak God's word to the body of Christ, so apostles can hear it and then work together with the prophets to see that word fulfilled.

There is a need to understand the gift of the prophet as well as the call and the rising in authority, favor and maturity into the office of a prophet and the office of an apostle.

5 Levels of Emerging Apostles and Prophets

Our friend, apostle Mark Tubbs, has written a very functional new wineskin book called *The Five Fingers of God*.[6]

In his book, Mark examines each of the 5 governmental gifts or offices in Ephesians 4:11-13.

He describes how each one of the five offices – apostle, prophet, evangelist, pastor and teacher, have five levels or anointings of development. Typically, every believer is called to function in the first level.

5 Levels for the Prophet

Level 1: All of us are called to hear the voice of God and follow it when called (Acts 2:17).

Level 2: Your gift increases and grace is given to hear the voice of God for those around you (1 Corinthians 14:3). This gift increases as it is practiced and matured with teaching.

Level 3: Your gift and grace has increased through an increase of your heart for whole cities and regions. Your prophetic words are given and received for these locations.

Level 4: Your gift and grace has increased for nations with global influence across the body of Christ.

Level 5: Office of a prophet. The body of Christ recognizes you in the Office of the Prophet and commissions you to function for the whole body of Christ.

5 Levels for the Apostle

Level 1: A heart for unity. This is for all believers. Jesus's prayer in John 17 was that we all be one and Psalm 133:1-3 tells us that where Gods people dwell together in unity, He commands blessing.

Level 2: Apostolic Anointing. It is a gift or grace given by God. The gifting increases and grace is released to lead others. This gift increases and is matured through mentoring.

Level 3: Recognized emerging apostolic ministry. Your gifting and grace has increased through functioning as a mentor and an emerging father to others.

Level 4: You function as a father/mother to the body of Christ. The fruit of your function as the apostle has increased – In your city, region and increasingly in your nation and nations and global influence across the body of Christ.

Level 5: Office of an apostle. The body of Christ recognizes the evidence of the gift over the life and ministry of the apostle by publicly commissioning them to function in the Office of an Apostle in the kingdom.

Being Established in Your Apostolic and Prophetic Mandate

My wife Cheryl has some wonderful insights on how prophets are established. She teaches that there are different ways people experience God and how it flows through your life to others.

Everyone has a different gift mix. You will have different gifts that will operate differently from others. This new wineskin gives people individual expression to be your unique self.

More and more, emerging apostles and prophets are learning how to activate all the body of Christ.

As we have shared from Ephesians 4:7, your unique call or 'metron' means that you have a unique sphere of influence that no one else has. So, you need to know where and to whom you are called. Your sphere of influence as an emerging apostle and prophet will reach different people groups, cultures and subcultures that no one else can reach. So be content in your unique sphere of influence.

When each of these aspects of your life, spiritual gifts, experience and anointing overflows together, you begin to find yourself fulfilling the mandate you were called by God to complete. This is called convergence. Convergence is a place in which you find yourself operating in the fulness of your calling and destiny.

There is an ease in following the flow of the Holy Spirit in fulfilling your destiny.

You might operate in this already and then the body of Christ acknowledges you officially.

Commissioning

Commissioning into the office of apostles and prophets is the official setting apart into your apostolic function by the body of Christ. It comes with great authority, empower- ing, and alignment for even more effectiveness in what you are called to. The body of Christ recognizes what Christ has done in you and the level of authority that you have already been functioning in for some time. In other words, man recognizes what God has already done in you and through you.

When apostles begin to function together and with prophets, they will shift the atmosphere of a city and region for God. We examine commissioning in more detail in Chapter 9.

Apostolic Centres /Communities

One of the new wineskins that God is using to do this is Apostolic Centres or Apostolic Communities like ARC

Global. Dutch Sheets said in 2001, 'I don't want to pastor a local church. God is calling me to lead an apostolic center for kingdom ministry.'[7]

God is transitioning the current church model into apostolic communities, hubs or centres.

Up until now, apostles and prophets have largely not worked hand-in-hand practically or functionally. While both celebrate each other, typically each type of office has functioned independently from one another. One thing is clear. apostles and prophets must learn to function more effectively together in this New Era. Part of this New Era is that we need to commission apostles and prophets into community!

We will look more in depth at what it means to be in an apostolic community through covenant in Chapter 8.

In this New Era, our commissioning and our sending must be done through community and covenant. All independence of spirit must go for you to be truly sent by God and 'Go' for God!

CHAPTER 5

How Do We Grow New Wineskin Apostles and Prophets?

There has to be a new understanding of new wineskin apostles and prophets in this New Era.

As 2 Corinthians 5:17 says,

'The old has gone; the NEW has come.'

For this to happen in this New Era, there must be great change in our thinking and hearts in how the Kingdom of God operates.

The good news is that this is possible. One of the best examples of changing your wineskin to a new one is in Acts 10 and 11.

Peter is in Joppa at Simon, the Tanner's house. He is praying on the roof of the house and goes into a trance.

Acts 10:11 says,

'He saw heaven opened and something like a huge sheet being let down to earth by its four corners. It contained all kinds of four-footed animals... Then a voice told him, '"Get up, Peter, kill and eat..."'

Peter objected to what the Lord told him, saying, I've never eaten anything unclean.

Then the Lord spoke to him a second time:

'Don't call anything impure that God has made clean.'

The Bible tells us this happened three times to Peter and then the Holy Spirit told him to go downstairs because there was someone looking for him. When he does this, messengers from Cornelius, the Centurion, are there to invite him to go with them to pray for Cornelius and the other Gentiles at another house.

Acts 10:30-33 tells us that Cornelius had an encounter with God, and He told him to invite Peter to his home and listen to everything the Lord had commanded him to tell them.

What happens next completely destroys Peter's old wineskin and pushes him and the body of Christ into a whole New Era!

As Peter hears what happened to Cornelius, he declares in Acts 10:34:

'I now realize how true it is that God does not show favoritism but accepts from every nation the one who fears Him and does what is right'.

And then the others with him in Acts 10:44 have the same shift into a new wineskin.

> 'While Peter was still speaking... The Holy Spirit came on all who heard the message. The circumcised believers who had come with Peter were astonished that the gift of the Holy Spirit had been poured out even on the Gentiles...'

There is a sequel to this new wineskin transformation story in Acts 11.

The leaders in Jerusalem had heard that Peter was now preaching the gospel to the Gentiles. Their immediate old wineskin response was to criticize him.

When Peter tells them the whole story in Acts 11:4-7 the old wineskin changes inside them too.

Acts 11:18 says,

> 'When they heard this, they had no further objections and praised God'.

It was a beginning of a whole New Era!

The gospel was no longer just for the Jews! It was now also for the rest of the world too.

An Era of New Wineskin Thinking

New wineskins do that. It challenges the old wineskin in us and pushes us to the point of change. But it is up to us!

> *The most important question for you in this era is, Are you prepared to change?*

Jesus's declaration in Mark 2:22 challenges us to change.

'No one pours new wine into old wineskins. Otherwise, the wine will burst the skins, and both the wine and the wineskins will be ruined. No, they pour new wine into new wineskins'.

We need a new wineskin. A place that the new wineskin manifests is in our thinking and mindsets.

New Wineskin thinking must challenge all our old mindsets.

So, once you have an encounter like Peter's with the Holy Spirit, and you have realized that you need to change how you see the Kingdom of God and the body of Christ, how do you proceed stepping into this New Era?

Remember, this New Era is an apostolic re-formation.

Thus, one of the major characteristics of this New Era is the restoration of apostles and prophets into everyday function of the church.

How do we walk towards implementing this change?

Mark Tubbs in his teaching 'How do we grow New Wineskin apostles and prophets?' will challenge the operating system in you. [1]

Are you willing to allow God to change you so you can grow into 'new wineskin' apostles and prophets?

Seven Strategic Characteristics that You Need to Grow into as a New Era Apostle and Prophet

1. Start from a Place of Love Honor and Humility

Honor is the manifestation of love and humility. When there is mutual honor, love and humility in a godly family, there is incredible blessing. This is also true for the family of God.

The greatest posture for any emerging apostle and prophet is to stay low and keep humble in your own eyes.

The greatest apostles that I've met today are the humblest. Apostles like Bill Johnson and Ché Ahn are some of the most approachable, generous, humble people I've met. They don't promote themselves. They know who they are and the authority they walk in. They seek to live each day in humility.

> *True new wineskin apostles and prophets model this new wineskin of love, honor and humility.*

It is this culture of humility that is essential for you to grow as an apostle and prophet today.

2. Jesus said there will be new order – a new design to God's family – Apostles

The first term Jesus uses in God's family is apostle.

In Mark 3:14, *The Passion Translation* says,

'He appointed the Twelve, whom he named apostles. He wanted them to be continually at his side as his friends, and so that he could send them out to preach'.

Brian Simmons, the translator of *The Passion Translation,* adds as a footnote to this verse:

'This was not simply a passive acknowledgment, but an active setting them in place. The Greek verb poieo is the verb 'do' or 'make.' Jesus 'did' them; that is, he imparted his favor, blessing, and grace to set them in place as apostolic emissaries for the kingdom realm of God'.[2]

If Jesus designated them 'apostles', what did he tell them to do?

He sent them out to preach the good news and He gave them authority to drive out demons (Matt 28:19 and Luke 9:1).

So, Jesus reordered the old wineskin. The first thing he did was to set apostles in their rightful place. In this new Apostolic Reformation, we need to do the same thing and realize that the new design to God's family begins with apostles and prophets.

3. How to function as an apostle or prophet

It is what you do that is most important. Your actions speak of your true values and not your words.

As discussed in Chapter 3, true apostles are not interested in a title. If you re-read the epistles written by Paul in the New Testament, you will see repeatedly he did not use 'apostle' as a title. It was not his name! It was what he did! He functioned as an apostle.

When I hear and see leaders using 'apostle' as a title to introduce themselves or others, it tells me that those leaders are not functioning as new wineskin apostles. They are still using an old wineskin model of hierarchy with levels of promotion, accomplishment and titles that they use to be recognized. Unfortunately, the traditional church is still enamored with this model of ministry.

True New Era apostles and prophets don't need a title.

The origin of the term 'apostle' is actually a Roman term. It is not from Jewish culture at all. The simple meaning is 'sent one'. Functionally, an apostle was a 'sent one for a specific purpose.'

This definition is important on many levels. The most important is if you have not been 'sent' by other apostles and you go on your own authority, you're not an apostle!

Typically, people have an orphan heart if they appoint themselves. This is the exact opposite to what the true apostles are in reality.

According to its original meaning, the true purpose of an apostle is to 'transform people to look or become like us'.

This is what the Great Commission of going into all the world and making disciples means in Matthew 28:19-20.

As apostles, we need to understand this mandate and do what Paul the apostle did when he said in 1 Corinthians 11:1:

'Follow my example as I follow the example of Christ.'

In the process, the main objective becomes to 'transform the world' by taking people out of the culture of the world and transforming them to live a kingdom culture lifestyle.

This was Jesus's intent when he called them apostles.

It was hard for the apostles to understand, but in Acts 1:8 he clarified it for us all:

You will receive power when the Holy Spirit comes on you; and you will be my witnesses....

Another word for the word 'witnesses' is 'martyrs.

A martyr is a person who willingly suffers death rather than renounce his or her religion; a person who is put to death or endures great suffering on behalf of any belief, principle, or cause. [3]

So, do you still want to be an apostle?

There is a cost involved. Are you prepared to count that cost and 'to lose your life' for the sake of the gospel and to transform nations?

This tends to take all the gloss off it for those who are ambitious and self-promoting.

It is going to cost you everything.

4. True apostles are apostolic fathers and mothers

When we first began our apostolic network in Australia in 2006, there was some resistance from national leaders who had been badly burnt over the previous five years. The problem was they had been manipulated by old wineskin leaders who had heard of the restoration of the office of the apostle and had re-badged and change their title but not their wineskin. Unfortunately, they were authoritative and hierarchical. They demanded submission and respect.

But true new wineskin apostles are not insecure or ambitious or in competition or have a control issue. True apostles are fathers and mothers who live to raise up the next generation of apostles and prophets and others of the five-fold offices of the body of Christ.

I still hear of orphan-hearted apostolic leaders who are ambitious, driven and self- promoting. If they were truly honest, they would acknowledge they seek to build their own ministry and not others in the Kingdom of God.

They have an old wineskin. They have an orphan heart.

And as I share in my book *The Father's Love – An encounter with God the Father*, unless you have the Father heart of God, you will struggle understanding this concept. [4]

> *In this new wineskin ministry, it is not about you! It is about others.*

True apostolic fathers and mothers all need to be mentoring, equipping and sending others out into ministry. Orphan-hearted leaders want to equip others only with the intent of holding on to those they equip so they will help them build their own ministry. They are not true apostles.

But when apostles and prophets grow up and become fathers and mothers, they begin to reproduce sons and daughters who in turn also grow up and reproduce others.

This is how the body of Christ grows in unity in the faith and according to Ephesians 4:13:

> '...and become mature, attaining to the whole measure of the fullness of Christ.'

This is what Jesus intended when he first called the disciples and then commissioned them as apostles.

A body of Christ will only grow into maturity when apostolic fathers and mothers mentor, reproduce, commission, and send apostles and prophets to do the same.

5. Apostles are foundational

When true apostles function, they are always foundational. Not top down but building from the foundation up.

Paul teaches us this in Ephesians 2:19-20; that we are God's people...

'... built on the foundation of the apostles and prophets, with Christ Jesus himself as the chief cornerstone.'

So, apostles and prophets are foundational.

They are not meant to be on the top of the hierarchy. They are meant to be the ground floor for the foundation on which the body of Christ is built on.

As Bill Johnson says, 'Our ceiling is your floor'.

This is the heart of a true apostle.

So how does this work? God's design is clear in scripture.

I Corinthians 12:28 says,

'In the church, God has appointed first of all APOSTLES, second PROPHETS...'

So, just like God intended there would be fathers and mothers in a family, God's intent in the family of God is for there to be Apostolic fathers and mothers

As we saw in Mark 3:14, Jesus appointed the 12 as apostles.

The Greek word for 'appointed' is 'to establish an order'. This is also in the body of Christ. Cheryl and I are the apostolic father and mother to an apostolic center in another city. We do not minister there often, but when we go there, so many of the leaders say, 'We just love it when Mum and Dad are here'.

I get it. Why? Because when a mother and father are present, it brings security and a sense that the foundations are strong and in order.

However, with apostolic authority comes great responsibility.

It is not power to control the lives of other Christians. It is what Jesus did in Mark 6:7:

> 'He had power to send them out two by two and gave them authority over impure spirits.'

One of the major characteristics of true apostles is their authority to transform lives when they preach the gospel and bring divine order to the body of Christ when they go into a new city, region or nation. But they are not just to demonstrate signs and wonders and bring order, they are responsible to create an environment or a kingdom culture where there is room for emerging apostles and prophets to grow with ongoing mentoring by fathers and mothers. This is the essential foundation that must be evident in the lives of true apostles and prophets.

With the foundational role comes opposition and persecution.

Our experience has taught us that you must be already functioning as mature apostles before you are commissioned! Because if we commission someone too early, the level of spiritual opposition will be too great for them to deal with and overcome. We have seen emerging apostolic leaders be commissioned prematurely only to experience spiritual warfare so great that their physical health, marriage, and family could not cope.

So, it is important to get it right. That's why the best way to decide who should be commissioned is by prayer and through observation over time by apostolic teams in an apostolic community or network.

6. The apostles and prophets are essential for the future of the church

Just like there is a divine order in a family, there is a divine order to the Kingdom of God.

When the church ignores the role of the apostles and prophets, it becomes weak and inward looking. And more importantly, it loses its influence on culture, the next generation, and the values of society. This is evident in the majority of Western cultures today where Christianity is no longer celebrated and honored. Those father and mother figures are now ostracized rather than listened to and celebrated.

Ephesians 2:19 tells us apostles and prophets are foundational in the body of Christ. So, we need them both! Not just on a local church level, but as mothers and fathers of cities and even nations.

Apostles are especially needed to increase and release the emerging five-fold next generation in the nation. You are never meant to grow and release yourself.

Prophets are needed by the church to hear what God is saying today. The role of the prophet is to teach the body of Christ how to hear the voice of God for themselves.

One of the weaknesses in the body of Christ at this time is people's over reliance on receiving a prophetic word instead of seeking God's will for themselves. Once you've learned to hear God's voice for yourself, the prophetic typically confirms that which God has already spoken to you.

In addition, when some people receive a prophetic word, they think it will automatically come to pass.

One of the roles of prophets is teach others that the prophetic word they receive *is an invitation to participate in their divine destiny.*

In other words, you have something to do. It is not going to come to pass by itself. You need to partner with God as you step into the fulness of His will for you.

It's also great to see national prophetic councils being organized around the world. Not only do they recognize those who are functioning in the office of the prophet, they also release the prophetic words that are for nations.

And they bring divine order when necessary. This is the New Era in operation.

> *The apostolic church understands who believers are created to be and honor and equip them into maturity!*

It is not enough to have growing churches in a city and your nation; we also need people growing in their five-fold office, so nations are transformed for the Kingdom of God.

7. Allow the apostle and prophet to function today

Once you cross the bridge and do celebrate apostles and prophets today in this New Era, then they need to be given opportunity to function within the body of Christ in practical ways to help introduce the new wineskin.

One of the key roles is the transformation of nations. I have been ministering in East Africa for over twelve years and function as an apostle in specific regions of Kenya and Uganda. I go there at least once a year there and sometimes more. African Christian culture gets the function of the apostle much more than the Western church does. As well as calling me 'the grandfather' to many apostles and pastors over whole regions, they also introduce me as 'the man of God'. They say it this way… 'The man of God is here!'

Not wanting to think more highly of myself than I should, I normally just thank them and quickly move on with the meeting. A few years ago, I had to make an unexpected trip back to Kenya to help sort out a difficultly in an organization that we mentor. Normally I travel with an apostolic team, but on that occasion I was travelling to Africa by myself. As my international flight landed in Nairobi, I heard the Holy Spirit whisper to me, 'The man of God is here'.

I knew exactly what the Holy Spirit was saying. The apostles and prophets as well as the bishops and pastors in Kenya had been pulling on my apostolic gift from overseas. Just like Paul's Macedonian call, I knew that my apostolic office was being called on. I knew I wasn't going there for meetings or even to solve a problem, I was going to bring apostolic transformation to the body of Christ and to the nation of Kenya.

Is this scriptural? Absolutely!

The great commission that Jesus gave all Christians in Matthew 28:19-20 was not just to preach the gospel, but to disciple and transform nations.

'Therefore, go and make disciples of all nations...'

This was the 'send' of the gospel! It is also the commissioning of the apostles to transform nations.

We are unable to do it in our own authority.

This is why Jesus say in Matthew 28:27,

"'All authority' has been given to me...'

To do what? Verse 28 tells us,

'Therefore, I am sending you...'

As we have learnt, the word 'send' here is Apostolos!

Jesus was saying, 'I am sending you to be apostles to transform the culture of people, cities, regions, and nations into a Christian mindset, lifestyle and culture.

This is what it means to make disciples of all nations.

So, the number one role of apostolic fathers and mothers in this new wineskin is to mentor, raise up and send others to preach the gospel. In other words, they are to disciple, equip and then send them out for the transformation of nations. This is the fulfilment of the Great Commission.

True apostles and prophets know who they are. They know what they are called to do and how to do it. They know that they have been commissioned by God and by their spiritual fathers as an apostle and prophet. And they choose to function whether they receive recognition or not.

They live to raise up others and build the Kingdom of God–not their own kingdom or ministry!

This is why we need to commission apostles and prophets and we need to send them out to regions and nations to function! I'll spend more time talking about commissioning in a later chapter.

The reason why this new apostolic wineskin is so important is because where we are seeing a true apostolic prophetic movement, there is true transformation in nations.

In conclusion, new wineskin apostles and prophets understand the need for Apostolic Alignment. God sets us in families. You need to know your family. You will read more about the power of apostles functioning in covenant relationship in apostolic community in chapters 9 and 10.

Most importantly are you growing in your new apostolic and prophetic wineskin?

This is now your challenge as we enter this New Era!

CHAPTER 6

The Heart and Values of Apostles and Prophets

Understanding the heart and values of apostles and prophets is so important.
Why?

It is wonderful to see more and more people catching a hold of the revelation that it is a New Era.

As this apostolic new wineskin is being restored to the body of Christ, many leaders are beginning to become aware that apostles and prophets are indeed for today and they are opening their minds to the possibility of functioning in a new wineskin.

However, as they start to adopt this new wineskin, some are progressing too quickly, without completely understanding the full revelation of this new wineskin. In the process, many are adopting the language, title, and even apostolic leadership model without actually understanding what the values are and how apostles function today.

More and more ministries are describing themselves as apostolic. This is a good thing. As leaders step into this New Era, we expect more and more people to begin to see it and want to function in it.

The challenge is that many are now adopting the language without understanding how an apostolic ministry differs from a church leadership structure.

As such, we are seeing a surge in the number of people who are now calling themselves apostles and an increase in numbers being commissioned by old wineskin to organizations.

While we are confident that eventually God will bring adjustment, this makes it even more important right now to understand the 'Heart and Values' of apostles and prophets.[1]

What Are the Things that Apostles and Prophets do?

Well the simple answer is they do what was demonstrated in the book of Acts after God poured out His Holy Spirit on the day of Pentecost.

In Acts 2 we see that Peter and the other apostles:

1. They preached the gospel in boldness with signs and wonders. After they received the baptism in the Holy Spirit they preached the gospel with boldness, and Acts 2:41 says that over 3,000 people believed and were baptized that day.

This was so unusual, that Acts 2:43 states that,

'Everyone was filled with awe at the many wonders and signs performed by the apostles.'

This was followed in Acts 3 with Peter and John healing the lame man at the Temple gate called Beautiful. In Acts 3:11, it says all the people were astonished and came running to them.

Then in Acts 3:12 Peter rose up boldly and said,

'Fellow Israelites, why does this surprise you?'

They go on to share that it was not by their power or godliness that made that man walk but through the power of Jesus Christ whom they crucified.

In Acts 4 we see that they would not stop teaching the people that Jesus Christ had risen from the dead. The power of the message they proclaimed was so effective that Acts 4:4 says that the number of men who believed grew to about 5,000.

Despite the threat of being persecuted and even killed by the Sanhedrin, Peter and John went back to the apostles and shared all the remarkable things that God was doing.

In Acts 4:29 -30 they prayed,

'Now Lord, consider the threats and enable your servants to speak your word with great boldness.
Now stretch out your hand to heal and perform signs and wonders through the name of your holy servant Jesus.'

They became even more bold!

And we are told in the following verse 31 that God shook the place where they were meeting, and they were all filled with the Holy Spirit and spoke the Word of God boldly!

After Cheryl and I stepped into apostolic alignment and were commissioned by Ché Ahn and the apostolic team at Harvest International Ministries (H.I.M.), all heaven broke loose for our ministry. Everything increased dramatically! Signs, wonders and miracles.

It started in Mozambique in 2008 where a deaf infant in his mother's arms was instantly healed in front of me, and then a young girl was healed of night blindness during a night crusade in a village in Mtwapa in Kenya. This was not just a few powerful meetings at one time. In subsequent months and years, demons would cry out and throw people to the ground as we preached the gospel, and more and more people were being healed. In Kampala, Uganda, a lady who only had months to live was dramatically healed of AIDS. We knew this to be true because one year later when we returned, she got up and testified that she was completely healthy and HIV-negative. So much so, that after six months of monthly testing, the HIV clinic no longer wanted to test her as there was no HIV in her body.

Now, maybe you've heard stories like these before. How Western ministers go to the Third World and because people simply believe, they are dramatically healed.

However, these signs and wonders are not just happening in the third world, they are happening here in the West too! It is part of the New Era! Signs and wonders will not be a rare occurrence in Western society and all other nations, but an everyday experience.

As apostles rise up in their apostolic authority, there will be a greater manifestation of signs and wonders like never before.

In this new apostolic era, it is not just the office of the apostle who will function like this... All believers will too!

Jesus said this to all His apostles in Luke 9:1:

> When Jesus had called the Twelve together, he gave them power and authority to drive out all demons and to cure diseases.

After the day of Pentecost, there were more than apostles in the upper room. In fact, there were 120 altogether who received the outpouring of the dunamis power of the Holy Spirit that Jesus promised in Acts 1:8.

Peter, full of the Holy Spirit, in Acts 2:39 declared,

> The promise is for you and your children and for all who are far off—for all whom the Lord our God will call.

It is for you!
It is your time!

New Era apostolic people preach the gospel in boldness with signs and wonders. In this New Era, we need to expect the unexpected!

In December 2019, Bill Johnson and Bethel Church in California prayed for the resurrection from the dead of a little girl called Olive. Bill rightly pointed to the biblical precedent of Jesus who raised the dead and told all His followers in Matthew 10:7-8:

> As you go, proclaim this message: 'The kingdom of heaven has come near. Heal the sick, raise the dead, cleanse those who have leprosy, drive out demons. Freely you have received; freely give'.

Bill shared that Jesus modelled and commanded us to the same. He set a precedent for us to follow. He went on to say, 'We are at that point, so we have said Yes!'

Even though little Olive wasn't resurrected, Bill said,

'This is our journey. This is our passion.... we have said 'yes' to this call.' [2]

This is an example of the New Era apostles functioning with boldness.

In this New Era, it will be a normal occurrence for the sick to be healed daily, people set free from demons and the dead raised back to life.

2. Apostles are called to permanently transform nations

The Book of Acts clearly describes how Paul and the other apostles fulfilled the function of transformation of every culture of every region and nation where they went to preach the gospel.

In Luke 6:13 the twelve disciples were named 'apostles' by

Jesus. As I shared earlier, this was a Roman term. Remember in Chapter 6 that the purpose was to turn people to look or become like us.

Apostle was a militant term.

As previously mentioned, apostles were not a Hebrew concept. It was part of the Roman empire's methodology for transforming the territories they had conquered.

As we have learnt, after a new nation was conquered, the Roman Empire sent in the apostles to change the cul- ture of the conquered territory to become a Roman nation in every way — culture, language, buildings and customs. This was why so many Roman marketplaces, roads, stadiums, and water aqueducts were built in cities all over the Roman Empire. Many of them are still standing today.

The apostles the Roman Empire was sending out were transforming the conquered territories to make them just like Rome.

They would send in what they called the Ecclesia! Normally, the term Ecclesia is used to describe the body of Christ, but in Roman times it meant more than this under- standing. After the battle was won and the new land con- quered, the Roman Emperor sent in the specialists in a fleet of five ships. The main ship transported the leader—the apostle.

Their purpose as a specialist or expert was to change people's lives and culture so they became like them. After the apostles had done their work, they sent in a Governor to maintain that new culture. See more in point 3 below.

Jesus had seen this firsthand. He took the concept of apostles and made it his own.

Apostles transform culture today!

Our New Era mandate is to transform the world with Jesus's culture of the kingdom.

These are radical words. The Great Commission of Jesus to us to disciple nations meant a radical response.

As a New Era apostle, you need to embrace the mandate to make disciples of nations.

In Matthew 28:18-20, the Great Commission by Jesus was first given to the apostles .

> *As apostles, you are called to fulfil the great commission and to transform nations. You need to have a transform of nations mindset.*

3. Apostles are called to bring God's Kingdom culture on earth

Why did Jesus use a secular term — Apostolos?

As mentioned above, after each new nation was conquered and the apostles had done their work, governors would then be appointed from Rome.

One of the main functions of governors of the Roman Empire that were sent to each nation they conquered was to make sure the transformation of the culture was maintained.

They had a responsibility to inculcate the culture. That is what Jesus intended when he used that same word and commissioned the 12 disciples as apostles.

The word 'inculcate' is not a word that we use regularly in the English language. However, it's meaning gives a powerful explanation of what the apostles' objective was as they entered each city region, and nation.

To 'inculcate' a culture means to impart, indoctrinate, instill, communicate, educate, inseminate, instruct, plant, drum into, shape up, work over, impress and even brainwash.[3]

You get the idea.

The Romans used apostles to change the culture of the conquered territory and nations.

> *Jesus was saying to the disciples and to you, 'I am not of this world. I want you to bring heaven's kingdom culture wherever you go'.*

When you now go to another nation, make sure you work with the emerging apostles and prophets there. Remember, you are not there for a conference or meetings, but to transform that nation.

Nations are transformed when you father emerging apostles and prophets by equipping them, raising them up and releasing them to go and do the same to the next generation of leaders in that nation.

Apostles transform culture to the Kingdom of heaven culture.

4. Extraordinary authority to advance God's Kingdom

In 1 Corinthians 12:28 Paul says,

'And God has placed in the church first of all apostles, second prophets, third teachers, then miracles, then gifts of healing, of helping, of guidance, and of different kinds of tongues'.

Why did Paul say 'first of all apostles'?

While this New Era is not about a hierarchy, there is a precedent of apostolic authority.

Jesus spoke a lot about authority.

In Matthew 18 there was a discussion with the apostles about the hierarchy issue of who was more important. Jesus challenged them to have a lifestyle of humility (we will talk more about this characteristic later) and how to deal with sin in the church.

He then made a powerful declaration in Matthew 18:18 regarding a principle that is important for the authority of apostles today.

'Truly I tell you, whatever you bind on earth will be bound in heaven, and whatever you loose on earth will be loosed in heaven'.

Apostles need to know their authority.

You have authority over the spiritual atmosphere. Once you truly understand how to bind spiritual forces and loose the Kingdom of God into the earth, you will have spiri- tual authority over spirits that bind people, regions and even nations.

This doesn't just happen. Like all spiritual muscles, the power to bind and loose needs to be exercised with faith until things begin to change instantly when you pray that way.

As you read the book of Acts, you will see Paul exercise this authority as he shook the dust off his feet when leaving cities (Acts 13:51), bound spirits over people who opposed them (Acts 13:9-12), and even raised the dead (Acts 20:10).

Authority for binding and loosing is also needed to bind the spiritual force over a territory to have true transformation over cities and regions.

Often this is because of historical sin over a region that also needs to be dealt with through repentance and renouncing generational agreement with that sin.

Apostles have authority to make extraordinary decrees for rain in the midst of drought; to shift elections; change spiritual atmospheres and transform nations.

5. Apostles work with prophets

Paul always made sure he had emerging sons on his team. First of all, he had Barnabas, then Silas. Interestingly, both were prophets.

1 Corinthians 14:3 says,

'But the one who prophesies speaks to people for
their strengthening, encouraging and comfort'.

Acts 4:26 tells us that Barnabus was known as the 'son of encouragement.'

This is exactly what he did for Paul when he accompanied him on the first missionary journey in the book of Acts.

He functioned in the office of the prophet alongside Paul the apostle.

Apostles need prophets to bind and lose and to know what decrees to make. This is why we honor prophets so highly at ARC Global and always begin each year in January with the prophets decreeing how to 'Start the year right' by decreeing the word of the Lord for thatyear.

Prophets get the revelation. But you need apostles to strategically implement it.

6. Apostles and prophets have a determined sphere of ministry

As mentioned in an earlier chapter, we each have a unique sphere of influence that only we, personally, have.

Ephesians 4:7 says,

'But to each one of us GRACE has been given as
Christ apportioned it'.

As discussed in an earlier chapter, the meaning of the word 'grace' in the Greek is 'metron.'

A 'metron' is a unique sphere of influence that only you can have. No one else can reach the sphere of influence that you have with the gospel.

2 Corinthians 10:12-13 says that each has a significant metron or sphere of influence, and you should not compare yours with anyone else's.

> 'For we dare not class ourselves or compare ourselves with those who commend themselves. But they, measuring themselves by themselves, and comparing themselves among themselves, are not wise. We, however, will not boast beyond measure, but within the limits of the sphere which God appointed us—a sphere which especially includes you'. (NKJV)

So, the question you need to ask is,
'What is my sphere of influence?'

What is my sphere of influence in my family, neighborhood, workplace, community, city?

Take some time and ask God to show you. You will be amazed the more you meditate on this.

As apostles, your influence may be even greater regionally, nationally, and even globally.

Regardless of the size of your sphere of influence, the significance and reward in heaven is the same...

Mathew 25:21:

'Well done, good and faithful servant; you were faithful over a few things, I will make you ruler over many things. Enter into the joy of your lord'.

7. Apostles are generous and know how to prosper.

Apostles lead the way in generosity.

How you handle money and whether you are generous are two of the key indicators as to whether you are ready to be commissioned as an apostle or prophet.

You have to step into a new wineskin of how to live by the principles of kingdom finance.

I can tell immediately whether someone is in the New Era or not by how they talk about money. Do they have money or does money have them?

One of the keys is knowing that God is your source, not others!

God is a good Father. Jesus said in Luke 12:32 that it is, 'my Father's good pleasure to give you the kingdom'.

You do not have to beg God. He is not withholding from you.

Here are some New Era principles for you to practice with your money.

First – Who is your source?

Be honest. The truth is most of us say God is, but we don't live that way.

I know, because it was just like that for us. For decades we lived in the land of 'not enough' or 'just enough'; never the 'more than enough' of Philippians 4:1.

Then my spiritual father challenged me that I had a spirit of poverty. Ouch! But I knew he was right. For me to truly rise up into this new apostolic wineskin I had to break out of the old mindset of how I saw money and provision and break into the spirit of generosity and freedom!

God must be your source. Not your income, your pension, your inheritance, your family and especially not other Christians.

You have to decide! Others are not your source; your wage or next honorarium or monthly support. Only God can be your source

Second - Cross the 'God is good' bridge every day.

Just settle it in yourself. It sometimes requires you doing this daily until you truly break through.

You must meditate and confess this until it becomes a mindset of your faith.

Then you can live a lifestyle of trusting God no matter what your circumstances or your bank balance says. To live this way, you also need to make this a lifestyle.

I knew I had broken through when I was out to lunch with a millionaire friend and the bill came at the end of our lunch. It was normal for him to pay. But out of my mouth that day came 'Let me pay; I'm loaded'.

I realized that my mindset had changed from a poverty mindset of not enough to more than enough!

This can be your reality too!

Third – You need to know how to sow and reap.

This is the key to the new wineskin mindset for raising finances by apostles and prophets.

We don't plead for support or go into debt.

We sow and reap!

The Bible says sow seed and you will reap a harvest. Genesis 8:22:

> 'As long as the earth endures.... seed time and harvest ... will never cease'.

So, the answer if you have a financial need, is to sow a seed and expect God to multiply it and to reap a financial harvest — Not put out a newsletter or a Go Fund Me page asking others.

No! God wants to be your source.

Does this work? Absolutely!

We have been living this way for many years and have ongoing testimonies of supernatural provision.

A most recent example was that my wife heard God tell us to take a strategic prayer strike team back to Israel, even though we had already been there that year. I knew that it was going to cost us more than AUD $8000 for both of us. So, we sowed a seed specifically for that provision. The next day in our ministry bank account we had multiple deposits from the Australian taxation office (equivalent to the Internal Revenue Service).

It was highly unusual for the Australian taxation office to be sending us money. What was even more unusual was that each deposit consisted of the numbers 7. One was for $7.77 cents, another $77; then $777 and so on and finally $7000 plus. All together it amounted to more than the amount we had sowed for the previous day.

No, it wasn't a mistake. Our accountant said they did owe us that money, but the refund had been delayed for over two years. Suddenly, it was released exactly at the point of our need. I know that was because we knew we had to sow first fruits and seeds in faith in order to reap.

'Honor the Lord with your wealth, with the first fruits of all your crops'. —Proverbs 3:9

You need to be intentional to honor the Lord with your 'first fruits.' Do you know there is a first fruits every month in the Jewish calendar? It is usually the first day of each month. So, you have at least twelve opportunities a year to position yourself for increase by sowing first fruits seed.

If you do, then Proverbs 3:10 says,

'Then your barns will be filled to overflowing & to your vats will brim over with new wine.'

The way to deal with the spirit of lack in your life is to sow a seed at time of your need.

'The Lord is my shepherd, I lack nothing.' – Psalm 23:1

You will break the spirit of lack when you sow by faith and expect a harvest.

Make it a way of life!

Ché Ahn, our apostolic father, teaches that apostles and prophets know how to prosper. He says the key is to honor God with our generous sowing, decide to live out of debt and ask God for multiple income streams

Most importantly, new wineskin apostles set the example.

The most generous I know are my spiritual fathers and mothers.

That is how a family should be. The fathers and mothers blessing their children. Not the children always having to financially support their father and mother. This is how the Kingdom of God is also meant to operate.

Apostles lead the way in generosity.

Apostles are generous and know how to prosper!

CHAPTER 7

Apostolic Alignment

In this New Era, you need to be apostolically aligned! Why is this so important? So you will step into the fulness of apostolic and prophetic authority and effectiveness.

One of the most frequent things said to those of us already functioning in the office of an apostle and apostolic authority is that 'I'd like to come under your covering.'

My response is always the same. While I understand what they are saying, I explain to them that the concept of 'covering' is actually an old wineskin term. If you have a 'covering,' it suggests that someone has authority over you in a hierarchy. But the new wineskin is not a hierarchy. It is not vertical. It's horizontal. It's heart-to-heart. It is primarily a relational heart-to-heart alignment.

Bill Hamon in his book, *Apostles Prophets and the Coming Move of God* explains it as a net. And everywhere there is a knot there is an apostle or prophet. And when we all work together in unity the net 'works'.[1]

So, alignment is more about finding other apostles and prophets who share your apostolic DNA and recognizing an apostolic father and mother that you would like to step into spiritual relationship and 'align' yourself with.

Is apostolic alignment biblical?

Absolutely!

In Ephesians 4:11-12 Paul says,

'So, Christ himself gave the apostles, the prophets, the evangelists, the pastors and teachers, to equip his people for works of service, so that the body of Christ may be built up'.

The word 'equip' used here is the Greek word *Katartismos*. It means to properly align. It is a medical term that is used to describe the procedure of setting a broken bone back into place. If you've ever had a broken arm or a leg, you would know that the pain immediately decreases when the bone is re-aligned or set into place. And the body can heal and become strong again.

As discussed in earlier chapters, one of the key scriptures in this new wineskin is Ephesians 2:20 where Paul says we are,

'....built on the foundation of the apostles and prophets, with Christ Jesus himself as the chief cornerstone'.

For apostles and prophets to be foundational with Christ, there has to be alignment in the foundations.

The foundations of a building are crucial. The most important stone is the cornerstone, from which all other stones are set into place and aligned. Once Christ is in place as a cornerstone, then the rest of the body of Christ should be aligned with Him and the apostles and prophets if we want the whole building to be built strong and stable, and for it to last for generations.

In this context, we see that God does have a divine order.

Paul shares this very clearly in 1 Corinthians 12:28,

'And God has placed in the church first of all apostles, second prophets'.

Apostles are mentioned first because they see the big picture and bring divine order in the body of Christ. Therefore, for the body of Christ to be functional, five-fold teams align themselves with each other.

So, there is a biblical precedent for apostolic alignment with apostles.

The Benefits of Being Apostolically Aligned

As well as being biblical and a new wineskin, there are amazing benefits of being apostolically aligned.[2]

When we decided to become apostolically aligned with Ché Ahn and Harvest International Ministries, our minis- try dramatically changed immediately. Within one week of our leadership coming into unity and agreement to align ourselves with Ché as our apostle, everything increased dramatically. From that week on, the number of salvations increased, our finances increased, and the number of peo- ple who joined our ministry also increased.

None of this should have been a surprise to us, as we knew that Ché our apostle had the gift of evangelism, had a prosperity mindset, and had such a remarkable international authority to transform regions and cities.

We advise people that when they align with us, then they also receive the apostolic blessing that flows through our apostolic alignment with our apostle Ché and Harvest International Ministries (H.I.M)

Some of the main benefits of apostolic alignment are:

1. Open Apostolic Doors

As apostles when you travel to another nation, you are not going to lead a missions trip or speak at a church or a conference. You are going to help transform the nation. For this to happen, you need to go through the right apostolic doors.

James Goll teaches that in this new wineskin you need to be careful how you enter other nations. Rather than going through traditional invitations from pastors or churches, you should only go through an 'apostolic door' that an apostle in that nation opens for you.

We learned this lesson first-hand in the Philippines in 2013. We were invited by a missionary to speak at a conference in the Leyte region. A friend of mine in Australia suggested that I speak for a church in Manila before traveling on to Leyte. I did not know that pastor, but I went ahead and organized the meetings. The pastor organized for us to stay with one of his elders.

The day after our arrival in Manila, the city experienced one of the worst floods in recent history. We awoke to evacuation sirens blaring. When we looked out the window there was over one meter (three feet) of water flooding the street, and the floodwaters were rising. Eventually, we had to be evacuated by an emergency rescue boat.

On the next day we were due to fly out to the Leyte region. As the plane was accelerating down the runway to take off, I knew something was wrong. I took authority over the situation. Then we heard a bang as if something had broken in the plane and it began to brake and aquaplane in pouring rain. Finally coming to a stop, I sat on the airplane repenting, because I knew I had not entered the Philippines through an apostolic door.

When we returned to the air terminal, I phoned the apostolic father I did know in the Philippines. I asked him if he would open an apostolic door for us in the nation for the rest of the time we were ministering there. He gladly agreed and things dramatically improved from then onwards.

I have never forgotten the lesson. And I practice this principle every time I go to other nations.

My encouragement is that you should do this too in this new apostolic era.

It is simple to do.

Just find out who is the Apostolic father of the nation or someone who has national authority as an apostle and ask them to open an apostolic door for you.

Jesus said in Matthew 7:7,

'Ask and it will be given to you; seek and you will find; knock and the door will be opened to you'.

Then you align yourself with their authority while you are in the nation.

This is very important. An apostolic door is NOT just an invitation from a pastor, bishop or large ministry or church. You need to find who the national apostles are in the nation. If they have a new wineskin, they will gladly open the apostolic door for you to help transform their nation.

2. Divine Order and Favor of God

The wonderful thing is that when you are in apostolic alignment, the level of divine order and spiritual favor dramatically increases for you and your ministry. This is our ongoing experience and testimony. We continue to align ourselves with our spiritual father in a practical tangible way, both through our financial sowing and honor; as well as drawing on our alignment in faith for favor and breakthrough.

3. Greater Spiritual Authority

Breakthrough and release came when I received the revelation of being aligned with the spiritual authority of an apostle. While everyone who is called can be an influencer, not everybody is functioning as an apostolic father or mother.

I have learned that before you can become a father or mother, you first must learn to be a son or a daughter of God.

In this new apostolic era, one of my first questions I ask after meeting other apostles around the world is, 'Who are you apostolically aligned with?'

If they can't answer that question, I know they are not functioning in a new wineskin. If they do have an apostolic alignment (and not just a membership in a denomination or a network), I ask a second question, 'Who is your spiritual father?'

If they don't have a spiritual father they are aligned with, how can they reproduce new wineskin sons and daughters?

The truth is. you can't lead unless you know how to follow. And you can't reproduce unless you first have a father's heart.

When these things are in place, and you are aligned, one of the greatest benefits is a greater level of spiritual authority in your life and ministry.

4. Increase in the Anointing.

One of the main benefits of apostolic alignment is the increase of signs and wonders in your ministry. You step into and live in a realm of a higher level of glory.

It is what Paul describes in 2 Corinthians 3:18,

'And we all, who with unveiled faces contemplate the Lord's glory, are being transformed into his image with ever-increasing glory'.

This is what every passionate Christian desires. My experience is that becomes a reality when you step into the fulness of the apostolic calling and your apostolic alignment.

Expect an increase in the anointing in your apostolic and prophetic office. It will be obvious to you and your apostolic and prophetic community. You will experience an increase in what Jesus said in Mark 16:17, 'and these signs will follow...' after you are apostolically aligned.

5. The Blessing of God

Another benefit of apostolic alignment is an increase in the blessing of God.

It begins and is maintained by the spirit of unity.

As Psalms 133:3 says,

'...when God's people live together in unity...For there the Lord bestows his blessing...

When we lived together in unity or align ourselves apostolically, unity and blessing overflow.

We have so many testimonies from apostles that after they are commissioned as apostles in alignment with us at ARC Global, everything increases dramatically. Typically, they experience an increase in influence, authority, breakthrough and blessing.

Apostolic alignment causes you to live in the overflow.

Practical Application

When you are commissioned as an apostle or prophet, you are co-missioned into an apostolic community or network. It is not a membership. It is not a title. It is much more than recognition by your peers. In this new apostolic era, you are commissioned into apostolic alignment.

How Does Apostolic Alignment Work Practically?

First – You need to be committed to an apostolic network or community

This is such a high value for our apostolic father Ché Ahn that he teaches that, 'I wouldn't join a church where the pastor is not apostolically aligned or under spiritual authority with an apostle'.

In fact, is so important that he won't allow anyone minister at his church or speak at any of his apostolic conferences unless they are apostolically aligned. They don't have to be aligned in his apostolic network, but they need to be aligned with another apostolic father or network.

Second – You need to submit to one another.

Peter Wagner states the core difference in this new (era) is clearly the amount of spiritual authority delegated by the Holy Spirit to individuals.[3]

This is both a blessing and a challenge. Because most emerging apostles and prophets at some time have been hurt by a leader with an orphan heart who abused their authority.

Anyone who demands you submit to them does not have the new wineskin. Remember the true spiritual fathers and mothers lead in humility from the bottom – not the top, demanding submission and obedience.

While we are all on a journey in dealing with our orphan hearts, as we come into the fulness of our spiritual sonship, there needs to be a clear value of leading from humility and honor.

True apostolic fathers and mothers don't need to demand obedience and submission.

When you are loved with the heart of God the Father, it is normal for a son and a daughter to want to bless and honor their father and mother.

It is out of this balance of the father heart of God that biblical submission is practiced.

The more you are loved, the more you respond in love and honor and the more you want to bless your spiritual father and mother.

So, submission is an overflow of the heart. As apostles and prophets, you need to know how to submit to one another.

As Paul says in Ephesians 5:21, we must 'Submit to one another out of reverence for Christ'.

Hebrews 13:7 says we also need to submit to authority.

Have confidence in your leaders and submit to their authority, because they keep watch over you as those who must give an account. Do this so that their work will be a joy, not a burden, for that would be of no benefit to you.

As the centurion said, 'Jesus, I am a man under authority'. Once you know your apostolic alignment and that you are under its authority, you also then have the benefit of that authority through your apostolic alignment.

It comes out of mutual respect and honor. Where there is true alignment to a spiritual father or mother, there is respect, honor and great blessing.

Is not a difficult thing once you have an attitude of honor.

Yes, it does need balance. But spiritual authority and submission to authority are basic lessons of maturity. I wouldn't make a major decision without seeking Godly counsel from my spiritual father or mother and other mentors.

In my book *Fathering a Destiny – Growing spiritual Sons and Daughters* [4] I share that as emerging apostles and prophets, we all need three levels of mentoring in our lives.

The first level is discipleship. It's obeying the great commission of Matthew 28:29-30 in going into all the world to make disciples.

The second level is peer-to-peer mentoring. Do you have other emerging apostles and prophets that you meet with regularly and have given them permission to speak into your life?

As Proverbs 27:17 says,

'As iron sharpens iron, so one person sharpens another.'

Who is sharpening you on a regular basis?

The third level is Fathering. The most important question is, do you have a spiritual father or mother?

Do you have an apostolic father or mother who is speaking to your life on a regular systematic basis?

If not, ask God for a spiritual father or mother.

Because He is a good Father, He will give you one.

You need to look for:

- A person you feel safe with and you have asked to mentor you.
- A father that you have made a covenant with.
- A father to whom you have given permission to speak into your life.

And most importantly, who are you mentoring systematically or a regular basis?

I always ask emerging apostles, 'How many spiritual sons and daughters you have?'

I'm not talking membership of the organization that they lead but next-generation sons and daughters who they are mentoring and meeting with on a systematic regular basis.

The truth is, if you don't have any sons and daughters following you, you are not a true spiritual father or mother.

Last - the Basis of All Apostolic Alignment Is Covenant

God is a God of generations – He is the God of Abraham Isaac and Jacob. He covenants with us from generation to generation. So, we must understand how to practice covenant.

Just as he sets us in natural families, He also wants us to be in spiritual families.

There were 12 tribes in the old Testament. They all had a different role and a different DNA.

In this new apostolic era, you need to find your tribe. Although you are welcome to be aligned with ARC Global, it doesn't have to be our apostolic community.

You just need to find your tribe in step into apostolic alignment with them. We'll talk more about that this in Chapter 8 – 'What is an Apostolic Centre?'

Most importantly in this new apostolic era, you need to be apostolically aligned.

If you are aligned with ARC Global you are apostolically aligned with Harvest International Ministry (H.I.M.)[5]

We have now commissioned many ARC Global apostles who will have their own apostolic networks and centers, and you could be in alignment with them within our wider community.

If you are not apostolically aligned, you need to ask God to show you who your apostolic tribe or community is and aligned with so you can step into the fulness of this new wineskin and this new apostolic era.

CHAPTER 8

What Is an Apostolic Center?

One of the things that God is doing in this New Era is transitioning existing ministries into apostolic centers. This is one of the major changes of this new wineskin.

Many are declaring that this New Era has moved the body of Christ from the church age to the new apostolic reformation age.

In 1999 there was gathering of apostolic leaders all over the world at the New Apostolic Roundtable in Pasadena. They declared that the New Apostolic Reformation had begun.

They recognised that not only was there a difference between the gift and the office of an apostle, but that apostles must also be commissioned by the Body of Christ on the basis of the fruit that has been observed. The church gives the office.

At that meeting C Peter Wagner said,

'God has begun to raise up Apostolic Centers or hubs across the body of Christ'. [1]

When God does a new thing, typically many hear the same thing because they have 'ears to hear what the Spirit is saying to the Church.'

In particular, prophets and apostles hear and perceive what God is saying to the body of Christ. When God shifts His body into a New Era, often there is a convergence of revelation, conviction and understanding of what God has done and our need to respond in obedience.

At the same meeting in Pasadena, Dutch Sheets said,

'I don't want to pastor a local church (any longer). God is calling me to lead an apostolic center for kingdom ministry'. [2]

Chuck Pierce subsequently decreed,

'God is creating a new model of kingdom authority and you are a part of it!' [3]

We are moving into a new wineskin, but we must always keep a biblical perspective of the old. We must keep a right humble attitude because God created the old wineskin too.

God loves the old wineskins. He does not want them to break. But He is not going to pour new wine into them. So, our heart must be not to damage the old wineskins.

So, one of the main new wineskin expressions is apostolic centers and networks or an apostolic hub of churches.

Alain Caron in his book *Apostolic Centers* says,
A seismic wave of revolution is about to shake our world with the emergence of apostolic centers. This is one of the most radical shifts for today's global church and the apostolic movements. [4]

What Is an Apostolic Center?

'An Apostolic Center is a beachhead for the gospel in a territory. It is a regional transformation center established to provide everything necessary for churches, ministries and the body of Christ in that region to grow and multiply.' [5]

In this New Era, God desires to form a beachhead in a region or a large city. For this to work effectively, a whole five-fold team needs to be operating across the body of Christ.

One of the mistakes we made early in this new apostolic era was to try and implement a five-fold team within the traditional structure of one local church. After 18 months of equipping and trying to establish an apostolic team, we failed.

Why? We didn't have all five of the gifts - apostle, prophet, evangelist, pastor, and teacher present.

Years later we realized what we were doing wrong. In the early church the fivefold team was never meant to be functioning only in a local church. It was always God's design that it could be across-the-board for the whole body of Christ in that region.

As Robert Heidler so powerfully teaches in his book, *The Apostolic Center,*

> 'How did the New Testament church operate in five-fold ministry?
>
> 'As I studied through the book of Acts, I found the answer! The biblical key to the operation of five-fold ministry was the Apostolic Center.'[6]

He went on to say the Apostolic Center was a teaching and training cent.

- A gathering place for celebrations
- A sending center for apostolic teams
- A resource center for the churches
- A place where even a small church had full access to five-fold ministry

The New Testament did not have large churches.

It was made up of hundreds and thousands of small house churches. Individually, each church had few resources. But these churches functioned powerfully because they were not alone. The churches in each region were linked to a central hub or center that gave them access to a fivefold ministry.

The apostolic center was in Antioch. Paul and Barnabas were successful in using this model in Antioch.

Acts 11:25 says,

> 'Then Barnabas went to Tarsus to look for Saul, and when he found him, he brought him to Antioch. So, for a whole year Barnabas and Saul met with the church and taught great numbers of people'.

So, Antioch became an apostolic training center.

Then in Act 11:27-28 we see,

> 'During this time some prophets came down from Jerusalem to Antioch'.

Why was this necessary? The church of Antioch had apostles and a teacher, but they also needed to be trained in the prophetic, so the apostolic center in Jerusalem sent prophets to minister there.

Thus, the five-fold ministry was becoming established in Antioch. Acts 13:1 says,

> 'Now in the church at Antioch there were prophets and teachers: Barnabas, Simeon called Niger, Lucius of Cyrene, Manaen (who had been brought up with Herod the tetrarch) and Saul'.

Actually Saul (Paul) was an apostle. So, they had the beginning of a fivefold team. Robert Heidler rightly observes,

> 'Once apostles, prophets, & teachers are in place, all the other gifts begin to function!'

Thus, by Acts 13:2, an apostolic sending center had developed in Antioch.

'While they were worshiping the Lord and fasting, the Holy Spirit said, 'Set apart for me Barnabas and Saul for the work to which I have called them.''' (7)

As a true apostolic center is a sending center, Paul went on to Ephesus, Corinth, Philippi and other cities.

In each city he used the same apostolic center model as they had established in Antioch. Why? Because it worked.

> *The truth is, apostolic centers are not new...God is restoring them to the body of Christ in this New era.*

Role of Apostolic Centers

First — They are to be used for equipping, teaching and training. In the early church, each apostolic center was begun by a visiting apostle for the equipping and training of new Christians.

Second–Apostolic centres equip and build the local church, but they must also be 'sending centres'.

Ephesians 4:11-13 is very clear. Christ always intended that not only should we be equipped; we also have to be sent out to build up the body of Christ.

A number of years ago, a friend of mine who was establishing an apostolic center shared with me that they were upset because one of the key emerging apostolic sons was leaving to go overseas to be equipped and join another apostolic ministry.

My response was 'You can't have an apostolic ministry if you equip and keep. You must always be willing to equip and send.'

Remember; the new wineskin is not about building OUR ministry but building the Kingdom of God as a whole.

Most apostles that I'm aware of don't really have large churches or ministries attached to their apostolic center.

Why? Because there are always laying hands on emerging sons and daughters and sending them out to establish God's kingdom purpose that is on the sons and daughters' hearts.

True apostles and true apostolic centres always are equipping and sending. Never equipping and keeping.

The model of ministry that focuses on building 'our house' is an old wineskin. It typically is 'my ministry' and 'my kingdom' focused —not Kingdom of God focused.

True apostolic centres are always sending out those they are equipping or who are aligned with them to other regions, cities and nations.

Why Are Apostolic Centers Important?

Because they fulfil Ephesians 4:13 and build the Kingdom of God until...

'we all reach unity in the faith and in the knowledge of the Son of God and become mature, attaining to the whole measure of the fulness of Christ'.

In the early church there was only one church in each region, so each apostolic center acted as an equipping and sending center where Christians had access to fivefold ministry gifts.

As a result, the then known world was transformed by the gospel.

So, on the basis of this example, no wonder God has restored apostolic centers today.

Ché Ahn in his book, *The Modern-day Apostle*, clearly describes many different types of apostles that function in the seven different mountains or spheres of society today. [8]

He believes that in this New Era, every major city of the nation of the world needs a major apostolic centre.

He takes it a step further by declaring that each nation will need to have a national apostolic council (like the Council in Jerusalem in Acts 15) to strategize the transformation of those nations. All the apostles in these apostolic teams are equal but all with a different authority and sphere of influence.

Since the Reformation, the structure of the church has been through different expressions of denominational structures.

Over the past 20 years, this New Era transformation has been taking place. Even though there are changes within denominations, the majority of the changes have been horizontal across denominational boundaries in the body of

Christ with the establishment of apostolic centres and networks around the world.

So much so that research now says that these apostolic centres constitute the fastest growing and most influential segment of Christianity today. [9]

Most importantly, we hear the Holy Spirit saying that we have permission to step out of old ways of thinking and old ways of doing church and into a new wineskin. Apostolic centres are a New Era unique expression of just that.

As an emerging apostle or prophet, are you leading or do you belong to an apostolic center?

If so, I encourage you to join to an apostolic community or a new wineskin apostolic network as part of this New Era.

If not, please pray about stepping into this new wineskin.

CHAPTER 9

Co –Missioning

This new wineskin is a radical shift.

Perhaps the most radical difference in this new wineskin *is the amount of spiritual authority that God gives by the Holy Spirit to individuals.*

As mentioned in previous chapters, this is a challenge especially for those who have been on the receiving end from orphan-hearted spiritual leaders who are supposed to be fathers but have acted in just the reverse manner. But the truth is that God has done this change, not man. So, there will be a new grace or anointing released for whole spiritual fathers to emerge who can walk in loving, humble authority.

As mentioned, in 1999 there was a gathering of apostolic leaders from all over the world at an apostolic roundtable in Pasadena, California. After spending a number of days praying together and waiting on God, they declared that the New Apostolic Reformation had begun.[1]

There was a profound shift in the understanding of the significance of commissioning apostles and prophets.

They recognised that not only was there a difference between the gift and the office of an apostle, but also that apostles must be commissioned by the body of Christ on the basis of their fruit from already functioning in this office. In other words, apostles must first be functioning in their apostolic calling and authority in the body of Christ before they are commissioned!

The fruit of the apostle is recognised first, then the body of Christ sets them apart for increase in their office.

Wagner goes on to say,

'The office is not given by the grace (of God). It is awarded by works. The works are the fruit of the gift over a period of time in the life and ministry of the apostle'. [2]

In other words, the body of Christ gives the offices of the five-fold by commissioning apostles and prophets, because it can be clearly seen that they have been already functioning in their God-given authority.

This is the right order. Commissioning should never come first. It is the recognition that you have already stepped into your apostolic and prophetic authority.

What does happen after commissioning is that everything increases – your authority, your impact for transformation, signs and wonders, souls saved and provision.

Like all new levels in God, it also comes with increased opposition and warfare.

Interestingly, the most opposition that we have had in carving out this new wineskin in this New Era is when we started commissioning apostles and prophets.

The truth is, most people don't like change. Especially those in church authority. So, when a new wineskin comes along and the apostles begin to lay hands on emerging apostles and prophets to set them apart to function in the fivefold office in the body of Christ, religion reacts, and all hell seems to break loose. However, as we already have had paid a large price for stepping into this new wineskin, we are willing to keep going no matter the cost.

Just be aware. There is a price to pay when you begin to commission apostles and prophets. And there is increased warfare that comes when you are commissioned. For that reason, commissioning emerging apostles and prophets prematurely is a major challenge. So, this must not be entered in to quickly – but in the fear of God!

Like all things new, most opposition is because people do not understand what this New Era is and what the apostolic alignment means. As Hosea says in Hosea 4:6,

'My people are destroyed from lack of knowledge.'

The answer is not to defend yourselves but to look for those who are early adopters of this New Era and new wineskin.

As John says in Revelation 2:7,

'For those who have ears to hear, let them hear what the Spirit is saying to the churches'.

What Does It Mean to Be Commissioned as an Apostle or a Prophet?

This new wineskin has highlighted a number of unique characteristics.

First it is fathering a next-generation mindset where you focus on sons and daughters rising up into their ministry. Not your ministry. So, when you are commissioned, you are commissioned as a father or mother in the body of Christ.

Second, you are commissioned into community. The practical outworking of apostolic alignment is that you find your kingdom family or tribe. When you know where you belong, you are then able to enter into that community through covenant. We talk more about this below.

Commissioning Defined

1. According to the Cambridge Dictionary, to commission means to 'formally choose someone to do a special piece of work...' [3]

Our conviction is that while the body does the commissioning, God does the choosing, not us. The commissioning process involves a long time waiting on God. In our case, the apostolic team of our International network were asked to pray for who should be commissioned. They all came back with the same names so they could truly say 'this seemed good to us in the Holy Spirit.'

2. Commissioning is also a military concept. In that context, it means 'to give someone the official authority to be an officer in the armed forces'.[4]

3. In addition, when you are commissioned by God, He gives you His authority and His apostolic function to do that very special work.

He has called us to do a high and holy calling to the nations! This means you have something to do that only you can do!

Apostolic Community

For ARC Global, the letters A.R.C. is an acronym that means Apostolic Restore Community (ARC). The word 'community' was chosen carefully and deliberately. The body was never meant to work alone.

Paul is quite clear in 1 Corinthians 12 that we need to be joined functionally with each other. Verse 12 says,

> 'Just as a body, though one, has many parts, but all its many parts form one body'.

And in verse 27,

> 'Now you are the body of Christ, and each one of you is a part of it. And God has placed in the church first of all apostles, second prophets...'

This is more than relational unity. Strategic unity only comes to pass when you are working in covenant with each other.

So, when we commission apostles and prophets, we commission into community.

God sets us into families. Both natural and spiritual families. You need to know who your family is! Another word for family is community!

Commissioning and the Great Commission to make disciples and transform nations were never intended to be done outside of community and covenant.

It must be done in community! All independence of spirit must go for you to be truly sent by God and 'Go' for God!

In this New era, we seek God and prayerfully seek wisdom as we discuss those who are to be commissioned over a period of time.

What does it mean to be Co-Missioned into Community?

God is building a new apostolic prophetic wineskin.

To be 'Co-missioned' is to be SENT out BY God and FOR God in whichever sphere of influence we have been positioned. In this New Era we *Co-Mission* in COMMUNITY and COVENANT with other apostles and prophets.

The biblical precedent is seen in Acts 11:19-27 in the apostolic center in Antioch and then in Acts 13:1-3 where

Barnabas, then Paul and Barnabus, are *Co-Missioned* together.

> 'Now in the church at Antioch there were prophets and teachers: Barnabas, Simeon called Niger, Lucius of Cyrene, Manaen….and Saul. While they were worshiping the Lord and fasting, the Holy Spirit said, 'Set apart for me Barnabas and Saul for the work to which I have called them.' So after they had fasted and prayed, they placed their hands on them and sent them off'.

ARC Global is a community of apostles and prophets that are *Co-missioned* to function in strategic covenant relationships so we can transform nations together.

If God says that a person is gifted and anointed for a *mission*, then we have a responsibility to send them out and *co-mission* with our practical support and covenant.

Instead of giving a title to the person's position or level of anointing, commissioning is meant to facilitate them, so they enter into covenant in their GOING and their capacity IN God to DO the kingdom.

When someone begins to emerge and function in their anointing, it is easy to see and will be confirmed by the body of Christ by the act of commissioning into community and covenant.

So there has been a 'new' apostolic key released – *Co-Missioning*!

It is the new operating system for the New Era!

This is a clear pathway to help develop you as you GO!

The benefit of this process is to help emerging apostles and prophets function much more effectively in transforming nations.

Co –missioned into Covenant

Most importantly, when you are commissioned as apostle and prophet at ARC you are Co – Missioned into Covenant.

God is the God of covenant. He is the God who made covenants with Abraham, Moses and with us through the New Covenant of Jesus's shed blood.

The concept of covenant is never an individual concept. It is always about coming alongside one another and entwining your heart and mission together.

When co-missioning functions properly, the great commission begins to take place with convergence.

As Ecclesiastes 4:9 -11 says,

'Two are better than one, because they have a good return for their labor: If either of them falls down, one can help the other up. But pity anyone who falls and has no one to help them up. Also, if two lie down together, they will keep warm. But how can one keep warm alone?'

And verse 12 reinforces the power of covenant in community:

'Though one may be overpowered, two can defend themselves. A cord of three strands is not quickly broken'.

So we are commissioning apostles and prophets to Go in covenant through community in their God-given anointing.

> *In summary, God is Co-Missioning us in community in this New Era for this Kingdom purpose.*

New wineskin commissioning and the Go of the Gospel was never meant be done outside of apostolic community!

Thus, your commissioning should be into covenant family so there is a long-term commitment heart to heart to each other in covenant.

In preparation for being commissioned you need,

1. A next generational mindset and humility towards your own calling is essential in the heart of the person seeking to be commissioned.

2. You need to deal with any issues of pride, arrogance, self-sufficiency and selfish ambition before you can be truly commissioned by God. As Paul says in Galatians 2:20, it is a whole new level of having to die to self.

3. You need to realize that you are not able to succeed by your own skill or knowledge. You are not being commissioned because you have the ability or gifts to succeed, but because you are willing to acknowledge your absolute dependence on God.

4. God will only commission you for the single purpose of saying 'Yes' to His question, 'Will you go for me?'

In this new wineskin, when we approach commissioning with this posture, God releases a new level of apostolic / prophetic authority for the New Era!

It is as Isaiah 22:22 says,

'I will place on his shoulder the key to the house of David; what he opens no one can shut, and what he shuts no one can open'.

At the right time, God will open the door of Co-Missioning for you.

Make sure you step through it in apostolic community and covenant. It is a clear path to help develop you as you GO.

At ARC Global we are committed to helping you to emerge, co–mission you into your apostolic /prophetic office.

CHAPTER 10

ARC Global's Apostolic Community

ARC Global is an apostolic community made up of apostolic people who are functioning as apostles, prophets, pastors, teachers and evangelists.

ARC Global has a motto,

> 'We know who we are, where we are going, what we are doing, how to do it'.

ARC Global vision is to be a community of apostolic people with real heart-to-heart relationships, no hidden agendas or self-interest. But it is made up of mature apostolic people seeking to increase theirs and others' effectiveness for the Kingdom of God.

In ARC 's formative years, God gave the leaders a vision of a revival well with a hollow axle coming up with a hub and spokes attached at the top. It was a prophetic picture of how

ARC's Apostolic community was to operate.
- Living spokes with revival anointing flowing to many apostolic centres joined together.
- On the end of each spoke there were connectors.
- Each connector representing an apostolic hub or center.
- So ARC Global is a hub of hubs of apostolic networks. Many of our apostles will have their own apostolic network and hubs attracting divine connections around the world.

ARC Global is called to help reveal, explain, and release this new wineskin so as to empower emerging apostles and prophets into this whole New Era.

ARC Global is a community where apostolic people come into strategic relationships through covenant and co-missioning together. The expected outcome is a substantial exponential increase of your effectiveness.

One of the keys to this happening is to work together at moving from relational unity to strategic unity.

A number of years ago, it was prophesied that this apostolic community was like a Naval Battle Group, all sailing in unison and formation in same direction but with different functions. Like a battle group, different ships have important roles. The submarines (watchman prophets) go out first, followed by the destroyers and battleships (apostles) with the aircraft carrier (the apostolic Centre or hub) which is the equipping and sending center. The other five-fold offices are represented by the other classes of ships. Each has a unique role and value. But together they are the most effective.

The power of ARC's apostolic Community is that it is Kingdom of God focused. The key objective must always be to build the Kingdom of God, not your own ministries. There is no room for the orphan spirit ministers who wish to build their own kingdom.

In the process, fathers and mothers will reproduce emerging sons and daughters who love the body of Christ and seek only to build it up too.

At ARC Global there is no room for self-appointed apostles and prophets whose focus is on their ministry. It is not about you. But about those who you are pouring your lives into!

Relationships First

The basis of this new apostolic reformation only works through heart-to-heart relationships. As we have explained in earlier chapters, is not hierarchical.

It is horizontal, not vertical.

Apostolic alignment is a key value which is understood to be very different from the concept of 'covering' (which is an old wineskin concept). Instead, when you're apostolically aligned, everything comes into a new level of transformation and authority.

Roles in Apostolic Community

The key values between each apostle and prophe in ARC global is love, mutual respect & honor.

There are leaders in the apostolic community. Their apostolic role is to come alongside each other through relationship and example, to show others how to grow a kingdom mindset, help bring freedom from the old wineskin in their thinking, as well as helping you equip and release others into this new wineskin.

The goal is for everyone to be released and flowing together strategically in apostolic community. And to create a community where people are equipped and sent with ease.

ARC Global desires to be a safe place where there are genuine, mature heart-to-heart relationships. Apostolic community requires adult relationships and maturity.

So apostles are needed to facilitate this community vision to have:

- Maturity that allows us to minister without agendas.
- A family mindset – we love and build each other for the common good of the community.
- A passion to hear what God is saying corporately and build the Kingdom of God together.

Prophets have an important role and prophetic voice in ARC Global.

The role of the prophets are honored and essential to see and hear what God is saying and to give prophetic direction to the apostolic community.

Apostolic people need prophetic people. ARC Global seeks to be a community where the prophetic is honored, freely functional and responded to.

ARC celebrates, equips, raises up and commissions prophets to the body of Christ and communities and nations.

ARC Global meets online, one on one, and together each year at our annual ARC community gathering. Here we celebrate each other's victories and encourage each other. Our celebration has a prophetic prayer and is strategically focused for this New Era.

ARC's community is a positive environment where we build each other up with apostolic alignment, strategic assignments, encouragement, equipping for growth, praying for each other. Our posture is to build up each other and bless the entire body of Christ.

ARC Global's Community enables the new wineskin; builds the Kingdom of God; commissions apostles and prophets; strategically prays; sows up; invests into this apostolic relationship together in community and covenant in this New Era.

ARC Global is a community of apostolic leaders & networks around the world with a 'New Era' DNA. We desire to build the Kingdom of God together through informal relationship and covenant.

> *This is who we are,*
> *what we do and how we do it!*

ARC Global is an international community of apostles and prophets who seek to:

- Rise up in this new apostolic era and wineskin
- Walk together in strategic relationships in community
- Build the Kingdom of God together
- Mobilise Prayer Movements in Australia and the nations
- Equip & send apostolic and prophetic teams to the nations
- Strategically transform nations together
- Father emerging next generation apostles and prophets

ARC Global does NOT have a formal membership but is relationship-based because it is a new wineskin.

To begin this apostolic alignment journey with us, you need to discover if this is your apostolic DNA by attending one of our 'ARC Emerging Apostolic Prophetic Gatherings.'

Please go to our web page at
www.arcglobal.org for more.

Endnotes

Chapter 1

(1) C. Peter Wagner, W*restling with Alligators Prophets and Theologians,* Regal from Gospel Light, 2010

(2) Bill Hamon - P*rophets and Personal Prophecy, God's Prophetic Voice Today*, Destiny Image Publishers Inc, 1987

(3) Bruce Lindley, Fathering a Destiny – G*rowing Spiritual Sons and Daughters,* Self Published 2nd Edition 2012 and *The Father's Heart – An Encounter with God the Father* ARC Global 2016

(4) Bill Hamon, *Apostles, Prophets and the Coming Moves of God: God's End-Time Plans for His Church and Planet Earth* Volume 1 of Apostles, Destiny Image Publishers Inc, 1997. Chapter 5 – 'Apostles Prophets and Five-Fold Ministries.'

(5) C. Peter Wagner, *Wrestling with Alligators, Prophets and Theologians*,Regal from Gospel Light, 2010. Chapter 9 – 'The Pierce Era Part 1: Establishing the Government of the Church.'

Chapter 2

(1) *Webster's Third New International Dictionary Merriam-Webster,* 2002.

(2) Ibid.

(3) C. Peter Wagner teaching on 'Apostolic Centers' at 'Apostolic Centers Arising', A National Consultation on Apostolic Centers, Glory of Zion Ministries 2014.

(4) *Webster's Third New International Dictionary Merriam-Webster*, 2002.

(5) Scripture in Song – Scripture in Song Recordings Limited, Dave & Dale Garrett, 1973.

(6) The 'adopter' categories were first described in *Diffusion of Innovations* by sociologist Everett Rogers in 1962. According to his research, there are five adopter categories—innovators, early adopters, early majority, late majority, and laggards. The early adopters are those who hear see and implement well before most. Then others grasp the new ideas much later on'

(7) Bill Hamon, *Apostles, Prophets and the Coming Move of God,* Destiny Image Publishers (March 1, 1997.)

(8) Bill Hamon, *Apostles, Prophets and the Coming Move of God*, Destiny Image Publishers (March 1, 1997) Chapter 2 p. 7.

(9) Bill Hamon, *Apostles, Prophets and the Coming Move of God*, Destiny Image Publishers (March 1, 1997) Chapter 15 p.237

Chapter 3

(1) Jenny Haggar is an apostle and leader of Australian House of Prayer for All Nations . See Judges 6:25-28.

ENDNOTES

(2) Bruce Lindley, *The Father's Love – An encounter with God the Father,* Australian Apostolic Restore Community (ARC Global) 2016, Chapter 4 p.1.

Chapter 4

(1) Alain Caron, *Apostolic Centers,* Arsenal Press Colorado Springs 2013

(2) C. Peter Wagner, *Wrestling with Alligators, Prophets and Theologians*, Regal from Gospel Light 2010. Chapter 9 – 'The Pierce Era Part 1: Establishing the Government of the Church'.

(3) Chuck D. Pierce, T*he Apostolic Church Arising,* Glory of Zion International, 2015.

(4) C. Peter Wagner, *Apostolic Centers Arising, Traditional Churches and Apostolic Centers* – A National Consultation on Apostolic Centers, Glory of Zion Ministries, June 2014.

(5) Chuck D. Pierce, *The Apostolic Church Arising*, Glory of Zion International, 2015.

(6) Mark D. Tubbs, *The Five Fingers of God*, Ascribe Publishing 2008.

(7) Dutch Sheets, As quoted by C Peter Wagner, *Apostolic Centers Arising, Traditional Churches and Apostolic Centers* – A National Consultation on Apostolic Centers, Glory of Zion Ministries June 2014.

Chapter 5

(1) Mark D. Tubbs, Teaching – 'How to Grow Apostles and Prophets', Harvest International Ministries (H.I.M.) Leadershift Conference, Pasadena, 2015.

(2) Brian Simmons, *The Passion Translation, Broadstreet Publishing Group*, LLC 2020

(3) Definition of a Martyr - Dictionary.com, LLC 2020

(4) Bruce Lindley, T*he Father's Love – An Encounter with God the Father*, Australian Apostolic Restore Community (ARC Global), 2016.

Chapter 6

(1) Ché Ahn, 'The Heart and Values of Apostles and Prophets', H.I.M. School of the Apostle, Pasadena 2010. Used by permission. And added to by Bruce Lindley

(2) Bill Johnson, Social media message on 18 December 2019, https://www.bethel.com/press/olive/

(3) Thesaurus.com, Synonym of the word 'Inculcate, Dictionary.com, LLC 2020

Chapter 7

(1) Bill Hamon, *Apostles, Prophets and the Coming Move of God,* Destiny Image Publishers, (March 1, 1997.)

(2) Ché Ahn, 'Apostolic Alignment', H.I.M. School of the Apostle, Pasadena 2010. Used by permission, and added to by Bruce Lindley

(3) C. Peter Wagner, *Wrestling with Alligators, Prophets and Theologians,* Regal from Gospel Ligh,t 2010. Chapter 9

– 'The Pierce Era Part 1: Establishing the Government of the Church.'

(4) Bruce Lindley, *Fathering a Destiny - Growing Spiritual Sons and Daughters,* Self published 2009.

(5) Harvest International Ministry (H.I.M.) – 'is an international apostolic network dedicated to discipling nations through church planting, equipping leaders, and catalyzing social justice. We believe that the world is ripe for harvest, as we witness God moving around the world. HIM is centered on the value of Spirit-led relationships, and we are excited to continue advancing the Kingdom of God together.' See www.harvestim.org for more

Chapter 8

(1) C. Peter Wagner - *Wrestling with Alligators, Prophets and Theologians*, Regal from Gospel Light 2010. Chapter 9 – 'The Pierce Era Part 1: Establishing the Government of the Church'.

(2) C. Peter Wagner teaching on 'Apostolic Centers' at 'Apostolic Centers Arising.' A National Consultation on Apostolic Centers, Glory of Zion Ministries, 2014.

(3) Chuck D. Pierce, *The Apostolic Church Arising,* Glory of Zion International 2015.

(4) Alain Caron, *Apostolic Centers*, Arsenal Press Colorado Springs 2013.

(5) Chuck D. Pierce, *The Apostolic Church Arising*, Glory of Zion International, 2015.

(6) Robert Heidler Power point teaching - 'The Apostolic Church Arising – Restoring Apostolic Centers', Glory of Zion International Ministries 2016

(7) Ibid.

(8) Ché Ahn, *Modern Day Apostles*, Destiny Image Publishers, 2019.

(9) Philip Jenkins, *The Next Christendom*, New Oxford University Press 2002 and *The New Faces of Christianity* New Oxford Press, 1996.

Chapter 9

(1) C. Peter Wagner, *Wrestling with Alligators, Prophets and Theologians*, Regal from Gospel Light 2010. Chapter 9 'The Pierce Era Part 1: Establishing the Government of the Church', p. 209.

(2) Ibid.

(3) Definition of Commissioning - *Cambridge Dictionary,* Cambridge University Press, 2020.

(4) Ibid.